Alexander the Great

THE REAL-LIFE STORY OF THE WORLD'S GREATEST WARRIOR KING

Nick McCarty

CARLTON
BOOKS

CONTENTS

BLACK SEA

MEDITERRANEAN SEA

EGYPT

ARABIA

Red Sea

TIMELINE FOR ALEXANDER THE GREAT

357BC
Philip II marries **Olympias**, mother of Alexander.

(355BC to 336BC Philip at war.)

343BC
Aristotle invited to Macedonia to act as tutor to Alexander and a group of his friends.

349BC
Alexander acts as king in Macedonia while his father campaigns against Byzantium. Alexander commands the army and wins his first battle.

337BC
Philip plans to invade Persia. He marries Cleopatra, a Macedonian. Alexander and Olympias exiled Alexander returns in the summer.

335BC
Alexander secures borders by victories on the Danube. **Memnon**, the Persian general, halts advances of Parmenion and Attalus.

356BC
Birth of Alexander at Pella, in Macedonia.

354BC
Philip loses an eye in battle.

342BC
Alexander persuades his father to let him try to tame a half-broken stallion. He wins **Bucephalas**.

338BC
August: **The Battle of Chaeronea, in which** Alexander commands the cavalry. After this Philip II is accepted as leader of **Corinithian League**.

336BC
Generals Parmenion and Attalus cross the Hellespont into Asia. **Philip is assassinated** and Alexander declared king. He is confirmed as the leader of the Corinthian League.

CASPIAN SEA

Aral Sea

Persian Gulf

ARABIAN SEA

INDIA

334BC
May: Alexander secures
Macedonian borders and
crosses the **Hellespont**.
Victory against Persians
at **river Granicus**. Takes
Halicarnassus.

333BC
March: Alexander solves
the Gordian knot. Beats
Darius at the The Battle of
Issus. Darius flees leaving
his family. Parmenion takes
Damascus.

332BC
Six month **Siege of Tyre**.
Darius makes peace offer.
His wife, Statira, dies in
childbirth as Alexander's
prisoner. *November*:
Alexander in Egypt.

331BC
Alexander visits oracle at
Siwa; founds Alexandria.
Defeats Darius at the
Battle of Gaugamela.
October –December: Takes
Babylon and Susa.

330BC
Winter: Defeats Persians
on the approach to
Persepolis. *May*:
Persepolis is burned.
Pursues Darius who is
killed by his own men.

329BC
Alexander reinforces his
army with local soldiers
then advances towards
the Hindu Kush.

328BC
The Macedonian army
fights a guerrilla war
against Spitamenes. He is
defeated. Alexander kills
Cleitus, one of his most
loyal friends.

327BC
Alexander and his army
capture **Sogdian Rock**
and defeat a leader of
local resistance,
Chorienes. Alexander
marries Roxana.

326BC
Alexander captures **The
Rock of Arnos**. *May*: he
advances to **Hydaspes**.
King Porus is defeated.
Alexander builds a fleet
to sail down the Indus.

325BC
July: His men mutiny.
The terrible march
accross the **Gedrosian
Desert**. *Autumn*: He
arrives in Pura with the
remains of his army.

324BC
Alexander restors **Cyrus
the Great's tomb**. Purge
of local leaders for
corruption Mass wedding
at **Susa** General Craterus.
October: **Hephaeston dies**.

323BC
May: Alexander mourns
at Hephaeston's funeral
in Babylon. *June*:
Alexander falls ill
with a fever, after
ten days he dies.

CHAPTER ONE

BEGINNINGS

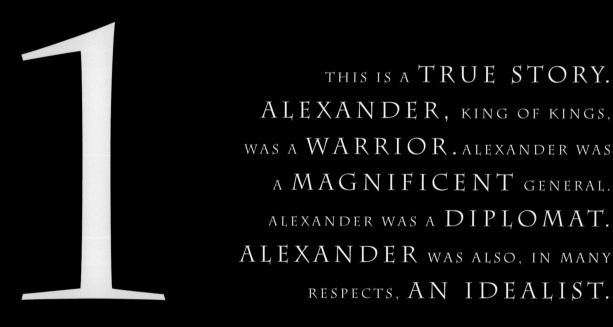

1

THIS IS A TRUE STORY. ALEXANDER, KING OF KINGS, WAS A WARRIOR. ALEXANDER WAS A MAGNIFICENT GENERAL. ALEXANDER WAS A DIPLOMAT. ALEXANDER WAS ALSO, IN MANY RESPECTS, AN IDEALIST.

ALEXANDER THE GREAT LED AN ARMY OF AS MANY AS 70,000 MEN AND THEIR CAMP FOLLOWERS FROM ONE END OF THE KNOWN WORLD TO THE OTHER. FROM 334 TO 323BC THEY FOUGHT EVERY INCH OF THE WAY.

THIS IS RECORDED NOT ONLY BY WRITERS LIKE PLUTARCH AND ARRIAN, BUT ALSO BY THE NAMES OF THE CITIES HE HAD BUILT AS HE MOVED ACROSS THE WORLD.

IT IS RECORDED IN THE BLUE EYES AND BLOND HAIR OF TRIBESMEN IN THE FOOTHILLS OF THE HIMALAYAS AND IN THE REMOTEST PARTS OF AFGHANISTAN.

IT IS RECORDED BY THE FACT THAT, FOR SOME, HIS NAME IS STILL A BLESSING AND YET FOR OTHERS, HIS MEMORY AND HIS NAME ARE A CURSE.

THIS IS THE STORY OF A MAN WITH A DREAM. THE DREAM OF UNITING MANKIND INTO ONE. HE TRIED TO ACHIEVE IT BY WAR, BY MARRIAGE, AND BY PERSUASION.

TO BEGIN, THOUGH, WE SHOULD START AT THE BEGINNING.

HIS FAMILY

To understand the history of Alexander the Great we need to begin even before his birth to Olympias, daughter of King Neoptolemus of Epirus.

The fact that she was not of Macedonian blood would have an important influence on her son's early life. Olympias claimed to be a direct descendent of Achilles, the hero of the Trojan Wars and the *Iliad*.

Philip II of Macedonia, north of Greece, was Alexander's father. Philip was descended, according to family legend, from Heracles and his military skills prepared the way for his son to achieve the greatness that he would subsequently achieve.

His brother, Perdiccas III, was killed whilst fighting an invasion by tribesmen on the Macedonian borders. Perdiccas left behind an infant son. Philip, 22 years old at the time, was made the child's regent.

As so often in Macedonia's history, this was a time of unrest. There were many pretenders to the throne: in addition, Athens and Thebes fomented trouble in the south and tribes continued to attack from the northern borders beyond the Danube. It was a time for decisive action and Philip was the man to take it.

He deposed the infant king and may even have had the child killed. In the power struggles in Macedonia there has never been time for the squeamish or softhearted. Philip II was certainly neither.

After taking the throne, Philip began to secure his kingdom. Bribery, warfare, threat and coercion were the weapons he used. He invaded Illyria, killed thousands of people in one battle, moved Macedonian populations into the conquered land and divided his enemies.

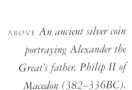

He married Olympias in order to stabilize his western frontiers.

To the sophisticated Greeks in Athens and Thebes, Macedonia had always seemed primitive and undeveloped. It was a land of harsh mountains and fertile valleys and life there could be very hard, but it was also a land that provided timber and grass pastures for horses, sheep and cattle. Fruit and grain also flourished in the fertile soil. These hard-working, hard-fighting Macedonians were entirely self-sufficient.

In Athens, Thebes and the other city-states in the softer south, the citizens regarded the Macedonians as barbarians, in the same way as they regarded all who were not Greek. They had evolved a way of

government that removed the power from a single man, or indeed from a small group of nobles, and devolved it to the people. All free people in the city had a say in their own governance. In such circumstances it was possible for great orators, like the Athenian Demosthenes, to exercise considerable influence on the actions of the citizens.

Macedonia, on the other hand, was still an absolute monarchy in which the king was chosen by acclamation. The king might take advice from time to time from a small group of nobles or an inner circle of friends. Traditionally, he was expected to listen to his people and could expect them to be very blunt. In practice, he wielded total power.

Philip knew that to be sure that none of the noble families were plotting against him, he had to find a way to ensure their obedience. This led him to create the Royal Pages. The eldest sons of the great and the good of Macedonia and the tribes he conquered along his borders came to court in Pella, his capital. They were there not only to learn the ways of civilized life, but also as hostages to their father's good behaviour. Thus Philip protected his back from the fierce rivalries within Macedonia.

It was Philip II who moulded the Macedonian army into a fierce and permanent fighting unit. He introduced new tactics for the phalanx, which revolved around a change in the main weapon of the infantry. The short stabbing spear was replaced by a spear 15 feet (four-and-a-half metres) long – this made the tightly disciplined infantry, who were formed up in a tightly packed square, almost invincible.

ABOVE *Ruins of the Acropolis and Parthenon, built in the fifth-century BC, situated in Greece's capital, Athens.*

MACEDONIAN ARMY

Philip remodelled the army. He had made it the most effective fighting force in Europe or Asia. He banned the use of wagons and only allowed a servant for each ten infantrymen or one for every cavalryman. The soldiers were expected to carry their own weapons, their own armour, utensils and some provisions.

The army consisted of three main units. The cavalry was often used as shock troops to attack the centre of an enemy unit at great speed or as sweepers to harass the wings of an enemy force, while the Macedonian phalanx took on the weight of the centre.

The infantry phalanx had been developed into 16 ranks, each 21 feet (six-and-a-half metres) long. Their spears were 15 feet (four-and-a-half metres) long and they attacked at a steady pace rather than at an uncontrolled charge. The spears of even the middle ranks protruded like a hedge of blades at the front of this advance.

The discipline with which the phalanx could be manoeuvred was formidable. They drilled and drilled until, on a signal, they could change from a frontal, open-order attack into a V-shaped wedge as they advanced. The military machine Alexander inherited was a hugely powerful weapon.

The army was also very flexible. Added to these two branches were the specialist bowmen from Crete and the men who commanded and built the siege towers for taking cities.

Philip's army could travel into the worst of territory at great speed because they were not encumbered by wagons or women. They could make lightening strikes before anyone had time to fear the event.

Some pack animals carried food for several days, tents, hammocks, medical supplies, siege machinery, loot and firewood.

With these infantry units and the Macedonian cavalry, Philip had created the weapon that Alexander would later use to conquer the world.

ABOVE *A relief sculpture of a Greek swordsman in single combat, fourth-century BC.*

RIGHT *Philip II remodelled the Macedonian phalanx by replacing the short stabbing spear with 15-foot lances.*

BELOW *A Greek black figure vase painting c.560–550BC showing two warriors using stabbing spears in combat.*

Macedonia was the protective buffer between the soft underbelly of Greece and the marauding barbarian tribes from the mountains north of the Danube. Philip destroyed the power of these aggressive tribes during various campaigns and also gave his army the fighting experience they would find invaluable in the years to come.

Within two years of taking the throne, he had secured the safety of his kingdom. By 357BC, he had taken the Athenian colony of Amphipolis, in Thrace. Gold and silver mines were plentiful in the newly conquered region, so the Macedonian king now had money to pay for his further military adventures. As he took more and more of the territory from the Greek city-states it became apparent that he was a force they had to reckon with.

In 351BC, Demosthenes gave his first warning about the dangers of the Macedonian threat to Greek democracy. His warnings were too late. Philip and his army took Thrace and Chalcidice, and the city of Crenides, where the apostle Paul preached more than 350 years later, was renamed Philippi.

DEMOSTHENES

Demosthenes was a great Athenian orator who continually warned of the dangers to Athens posed by the growing power of Macedonia. Philip took little notice of these verbal attacks, but the speeches made against him (known as "The Philippics") provide some of the most powerful speeches ever made in Ancient Greek history. Demosthenes offered practical help to the Thebans by providing them with arms when they stood against the Macedonians.

When Alexander succeeded his father, Demosthenes told the Athenians that Alexander was a braggart and of no consequence. He persuaded the Greeks to depose Alexander from his leadership of the Greek League. It was an error Demosthenes came to regret.

As Aeschines wrote as the battle of Issus was being fought:

"You, Demosthenes, claimed Alexander would be destroyed by the Persian cavalry. Our city wasn't big enough to contain your boastfulness. You pranced about mocking me as a bull ready for the sacrifice, with gilded horns and garlands, whenever anything happened to Alexander ..."

Despite Demosthenes' political failure and his failure on the battlefield, he was a great and powerful orator with an overriding hatred of the way Macedonian kings wielded their power. Demosthenes believed in a limited democracy.

INSET *Demosthenes the great Athenian orator and sworn enemy of Philip II and Alexander the Great.*

By the time Philip had taken Phocis in 346BC, Macedonia was part of the Amphictyonic League and had a voice in Greek politics. When he went on to defeat the combined forces of Athens and Thebes in 338BC, Philip became the master of Greece.

It was time for him to begin his great adventure – to free cities founded by Greeks along the Anatolian coastline from Persian rule and to take on the Persian Empire. He was too late. At a wedding to celebrate another dynastic marriage, an assassin's blade slaughtered him.

He left a son, Alexander. And already, Alexander had a dream.

ALEXANDER'S BIRTH
AND CHILDHOOD

Who was this 20-year-old youth made king by acclamation on the day of his father's assassination?

From the time of Alexander's conception there had been omens about him. There was thunder and lightning in the air when he was conceived.

Plutarch wrote: "On the night before the marriage was consummated, the bride dreamed that a thunderbolt fell upon her belly, which kindled a great fire and that the flame extended itself far and wide before it disappeared."

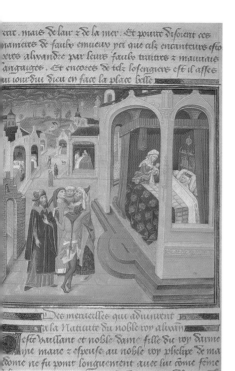

It is true that Olympias was a strange and powerful woman. In the Macedonian court, a powerful personality in the favoured wife was essential because the king was allowed many wives and the struggle for succession was never-ending. To provide the first-born son was one thing, but to provide a son powerful enough to take the royal role was quite another.

Olympias, though not Macedonian by birth, was determined that her son would be the one to assume the royal role. She was reputed to be deeply involved in an Orphic cult and to be an initiate of the orgiastic rites of Dionysus. It was said that Olympias sometimes became possessed by the spirit of the god. She introduced the handling of large and dangerous snakes into the rites.

This was the strange and powerful woman who gave birth to Alexander. Some time after the marriage, Philip dreamed that he saw himself sealing up his wife's womb using the royal seal of a lion. The soothsayers told him he should watch her carefully. Only one soothsayer said that his dream meant that she was pregnant and about to bring forth a son as bold as a lion.

This woman, and the stories about her, worried, and maybe even frightened, Philip, for he no longer kept her close to him. They called their son Alexander, and he lived with the royal court in Pella.

Pella was a city which at one time stood close by the sea. Fine mosaic floors still remain in the recently excavated palace. It was a rich and energetic city. Even before Philip took the crown, men like Hippocrates, Pindar and Euripides, lived in the court. It was no "barbarian" city, whatever the Athenians may have thought. The royal family lived in a palace created by Zeuxis, one of the greatest architects of the time.

Philip was a practical man. A statesman, a man Machiavelli approved of. He was a drinker, a lover of beautiful women and above all a great soldier. He had a powerful body as befits a master of arms. His face was broad, his beard and hair curled in the fashion of the time. In one battle it is said he had lost his eye to a bowman. He vowed if he ever caught the bowman he would be hanged from the highest of trees. History, however, does not record whether the archer was ever captured.

Alexander certainly inherited his father's drive, his determination and above all his understanding of how to treat his men – in short, he inherited his father's knowledge of how to lead. These lessons and the new army were his father's greatest gifts to his son.

Philip was not only a fine soldier – he was also something of a diplomat. He ensured that Pella continued to be filled with powerful political figures from around the known world. Men who had left Persia, because they were being persecuted, were particularly welcome, as they brought knowledge and intelligence about the empire Philip dreamed of conquering. Despite his warlike nature, Philip always welcomed poets, writers, philosophers and diplomats from the Greek cities into his court. As a result, Alexander grew up with a knowledge of the great literature of the Hellenic age, of music and dance as well as the arts of war.

In 342BC, when he was 14, Alexander's father asked Plato's pupil, Aristotle, to come to Macedonia to teach not only Alexander but also a small and select group of young men who would be the core of Alexander's future friends and commanders. They lived and learned together in a house in a village called Mieza.

ARISTOTLE

Aristotle was the son of a Greek doctor who had served at the court of Philip II. His father encouraged him in his studies and, at the age of 18, he went to Athens to study under Plato. He stayed in Plato's school for 20 years until Plato's death in 347BC. He rejected abstract ideas in favour of verifiable facts. Happiness, he taught, can best be achieved by finding a point between two extremes – balance is all; moderation in all things; courage over rashness; control over passion. For Aristotle, a man in a state of passion was just the same as a man asleep, drunk or insane. His belief in religion was based not on a God or gods who intervened in the affairs of man. Nor did he believe that the gods created the Earth. For him, the world had existed since eternity.

He taught Alexander that the state existed to promote moderation and to protect the individual from abuse. The state must always offer its free citizens a great measure of liberty. These ideas of balance and fairness would guide Alexander's behaviour in the future.

In Aristotle's view, the best training for young men was to be a warrior! This must have been music to the ears of the youthful Alexander and his young companions in the school at Mieza.

INSET *Aristotle teaching his young pupil, Alexander. From a painting by J.L.G. Ferris.*

WHAT DID ALEXANDER LOOK LIKE AT THIS TIME?

Plutarch described Alexander thus:

"the statues of Lysippus were the best likenesses. The turn of his head which leaned a little to one side and the quickness of his eye were best hit off by that artist. Apelles painted him in the character of Jupiter armed with thunder but did not succeed with his complexion making his skin too brown. There was a tinge of red in his face and upon his breast. His breath and body were so fragrant that they perfumed his undergarments."

Arrian, the historian, described him as "well built but not above average height. His eyes," he said, "were of different colours. One was dark as night and the other blue as blackbirds' eggs. He stood with his head cocked a little to one side as if asking a question."

He was certain of his place in the world. Once, when his companions asked him if he was going to run in the races at a celebration, he said he would only run if it was against kings.

Here was a young man open to the ideas and the powerful personality of one of the greatest minds the world has ever known. Aristotle taught by argument and discussion, just as he had been taught by Plato.

The temple of the Nymphs at Mieza, 18-and-a-half miles (30 kilometres) from Pella, was in a quiet and lovely part of Macedonia. There, removed from the court, Aristotle ranged his teaching across many disciplines and encouraged Alexander's enquiring mind.

Aristotle was also a great healer and often treated his friends when they were ill. He passed on this knowledge to Alexander, as well as discussing philosophy, the nature of leadership, happiness, religion, zoology, classification, botany, biology, logic and art.

He also gave Alexander an abiding love for the work of Homer and the *Iliad*, Homer's epic poem about the Trojan war and Alexander's ancestor, Achilles. This was a book Alexander took with him wherever he led his armies.

While he was being educated, his father, Philip, went on winning battles and capturing cities. Alexander was afraid, he told his friends, that if his father continued like this, he would leave nothing left for him to conquer.

STORIES ABOUT THE YOUNG MAN

Inevitably stories began to be told about this charismatic young man. There was a story from the Caucasus concerning his birth.

When he was born, the story went, he immediately began to run. He ran first to one corner of the room, then turned and ran to the next corner and there he turned and ran to the next corner. He turned and an angel stood in his way and, knocking him down, stopped him from running to the last corner.

The storyteller tells us that this happened so that Alexander would understand that while most things he wanted he would achieve ... there would always be something that would stay out of his reach.

Perhaps one of the best-known stories illustrates how the young Alexander already displayed the signs of diplomatic skill, self-confidence, physical bravery and a willingness to gamble that would be the basis of his future.

BUCEPHALUS

Horses were beloved by Macedonians and by Philip in particular. Traders from Arabia and all over the world came to the court in Pella with their best and most powerful animals, for Philip was known to be a lover of horses and was also a generous man.

One morning a horse dealer came to the court and sold a string of stallions. By noon he was left with only one animal – he pleaded with the men who had gathered round to buy it: "This is a special animal. He is of such breeding as the horses of the gods are come from. This is a horse for a great warrior."

"And no doubt has a price to match," scoffed one of the men near the king.

The trader looked at the men and then directly at Philip and said: "For such a horse there is no price. But for you I will sell him at 13 talents." It was a considerable amount of gold.

Philip heard this and laughed. "A king's ransom for a horse?" he said.

Philip had enough horses and now he was being tempted by a salesman from a distant land of plains and dark, purple-shadowed mountains.

The courtiers and the military men knew their king. He would not be able to resist. The horse trader smiled. He knew it also.

"Very well … Bring him to the flat plain by the river. We'll have a look at him."

The horse was magnificent. Powerful quarters, arched neck, pricked ears, and eyes that looked everywhere. He skittered sideways as the man on the lead rein brought him from the shadows under the trees. His lips drew back over large teeth. He snorted and tossed his head.

Philip and his friends watched. Alexander stood aside from the men of the court and watched also. He was 14 years old and knew his place was to stay silent amongst such powerful men.

The horse dealer went on: "Tireless on the flat, brave over broken country. He needs strong hands and brave ones. My lords, here is a horse fit for only the bravest of men. Who will try him?"

One of the king's friends looked towards Philip who smiled and nodded.

"Why not, my friend. I have enough horses. Though he looks a lively animal." He knew it did no harm to appear uninterested.

The friend walked out into the bright light of the early afternoon and dropped his cloak to the ground. He stepped across to the groom holding the leading rein and went to vault straight onto the quivering animal's back.

The horse bolted sideways and Philip's friend fell cursing to the ground. The horse would have stomped on the fallen man had it not been for the speed of the groom, who grabbed the leading rein and hauled the wildly plunging animal aside. Philip looked at the horse dealer, who shrugged.

"I said he needed strong hands, my lord," he said.

"I'll try him," said another of the king's friends. He managed to mount the horse. Then the horse arched his back, flung his legs sideways like a crab and slammed down and bucked at the same time. The rider went clear over the horse's head onto the ground.

The horse stood quivering, nostrils flaring and foam at his mouth.

"How much did you want for this unbroken killer?" asked Philip.

The horse dealer shrugged. "I gave you the price, majesty. Thirteen talents, my lord."

At this the men roared with laughter and Philip shook his head.

"That's enough to buy me 1,000 soldiers for a year. Do we look like fools? Take that stallion away and never come back to sell us such things again."

"Father," said Alexander, quietly. He stepped out of the shadow cast by the trees in the mid-afternoon sunshine.

"Father, they are losing a great horse just because they don't know how to handle him … or dare not."

Philip was angry and ashamed at his son's rudeness to his elders. The courtiers were not pleased to be called cowards, even if it was by the king's son.

Philip snapped at the boy. "Do you dare find fault with your elders because you think you know more than they do?"

"I can ride that horse."

Alexander stood his ground. Philip shook his head. He was afraid the boy would be hurt.

"You shall not. He's too dangerous."

"I will ride him. If I do, will you pay for him? I can ride him, father. Will you pay the price if I do?"

King Philip was torn between pride and anger. Pride that his first-born son was bold enough to take on such a wild animal and anger that he and his friends were being mocked by one of his children.

"And when he throws you off? If he doesn't trample you to death what will you pay me?"

"He is worth the price, father. I will find a way and I will pay you 13 talents."

At that the others laughed again. Philip looked closely at his determined son and, after a moment, nodded. "Do it then, boy."

Alexander walked quietly to the horse and reached very slowly for the leading rein. All the time he talked softly to the animal. Then he walked him slowly in a half circle, until the horse could no longer see his own shadow. The horse stopped flicking and juddering ... He calmed down very slowly. Eventually he was still.

ABOVE *Alexander tames Bucephalus, which means Ox Head, the wild horse he asked his father Philip to pay for.*

Alexander reached around his neck to hold him gently. Carefully, he turned and lightly vaulted onto the back of the horse. For a moment it stood as if transfixed and then it broke into a gallop straight along the plain.

It thundered into the pale distance. It looked as if it would gallop off the end of the world.

The men watched eagerly and none more so than King Philip, who was proud of the boy on the horse's back. There was danger yet from a half-tamed animal like this one.

Slowly ... slowly, Alexander turned the horse around and equally slowly he reined in the animal until it was walking. He stopped the horse near his father and the now-silent, open-mouthed men. He dismounted and leaned into the horse's face and blew softly into its nostrils. The horse laid its head for a moment on the boy's shoulder.

The men burst into applause. Philip embraced the boy.

Plutarch recorded that his proud father said: "My boy, you must find a Kingdom big enough for your ambition. Macedonia is too small for you."

That night, Alexander told his mother that he had seen the horse was frightened by the shadow it cast on the ground. All he had done was move the horse so that it could no longer see the shadow. The rest was simple.

"No, oh no, my boy. The rest was courage and daring to risk all. That is destiny my son."

He also told her what his father had said. Olympias was worried, for she could read his father well. "Beware, now, of your father," she said and kissed him.

The horse was called Bucephalus, meaning "Ox Head", which was the shape of the brand burned on its shoulder by the Thessalian breeders. And Bucephalus carried Alexander for the next 17 years as far as India and even there he is still remembered.

EXILE

Philip had taken a number of wives to cement alliances and to ensure the safety of his kingdom. Polygamy was permitted for the King of Macedonia. These wives lived in separate quarters in the palace at Pella and inevitably they were jealous of each other as they plotted to position their children favourably in the line of succession. Their squabbles and jealousies caused a great deal of trouble in the court.

Olympias was particularly difficult and very protective of her son and of what she regarded as his rightful position. She was also as ruthless as an ambitious woman can be. There were times when she tried to cause a division between her husband and her son. The old lion and the cub.

In 337BC, Attalus, one of the most influential nobles at court, took a hand in these women's arguments. He persuaded Philip that the only way for the Macedonian kingdom to hold together after his death would be to cement it by marrying and having an heir who was of pure Macedonian blood. Olympias was not a Macedonian.

It was hardly the act of a disinterested man, Attalus had calculated every move. He just happened to be the uncle of a girl of impeccable pedigree. Cleopatra was young and beautiful, but above all else, she was Macedonian and was made available for the old, battle-scarred, one-eyed king.

The tension between Philip and Alexander was fuelled to boiling point during the preparations for the inevitable marriage. Olympias was wild with jealousy. The habit of most men at a wedding feast was to drink too much unwatered wine. It may be that this was the case on this occasion. It may be that Attalus, seeing Alexander as a block to his ambitions, deliberately inflamed an already unstable situation. At the marriage feast emotions boiled over and Attalus was the cause.

Rising from his couch, Attalus stood with a golden goblet in his hand and proposed that all Macedonians pray to the gods that the marriage of Philip and his niece, Cleopatra, might result in a legitimate Macedonian heir to the throne.

It could hardly be expected that Alexander, who believed himself to be that heir, should accept such an insult to his legitimacy. In a drunken fury he stood up crying out: "You dare call me a bastard, do you?!" and flung his drinking cup at Attalus. In a moment the hall was in an uproar. Some of the young men in the room laughed at the sight of Attalus soaked with wine. The older men were shocked and angered by Alexander's actions. He had been deliberately provoked by Attalus, but a young man was meant to treat his elders with respect. Alexander stood shaking with anger as he faced Attalus. He expected Attalus to respond but it was not Attalus who reprimanded him.

Philip was undoubtedly besotted by the young girl he was about to take to his bed – he staggered to his feet. Plutarch describes the scene: "Drawing his sword he lurched towards his unarmed son. He was so drunk that he tripped and sprawled on the floor. Alexander stood over his father and jeered at him ... 'Here's the man who is preparing to cross from Europe into Asia and he can't even cross from one table to another without falling over.'"

It was a dangerous remark and Alexander was lucky to escape with his life.

The insult to his father made the situation too dangerous for either Alexander or his mother and they both fled from Pella. Alexander took his mother to her home in Epirus and then went on to Illyria.

It seemed that Attalus had made his move at exactly the right time. His niece was now married to a king planning a dangerous military campaign into Asia. Fate might take a hand for Attalus.

It all seemed to be a wonderful chance for an ambitious man to seize power, should the right moment arise. All Cleopatra had to do was have a son.

Alexander had forgotten one of Aristotle's precepts. That a man overcome by drink is no better than a lunatic. Alexander's star seemed to be waning. At the age of 16, Alexander was left by his father to rot in exile.

CHAPTER TWO

THREATS

IF ALEXANDER WAS TO TAKE ANY FURTHER PART IN HIS FATHER'S PLANS TO INVADE ASIA HE NEEDED TO RETURN TO COURT. HOWEVER, HE WAS A STUBBORN YOUNG MAN – HE WOULD WAIT TO BE ASKED.

KING PHILIP'S AMBITION TO CROSS THE HELLESPONT
AND LEAD HIS ARMY INTO THE PERSIAN EMPIRE RELIED ON HAVING A
SECURE BASE. HE CONTINUED TO FIGHT AND HARRY THE
TROUBLESOME TRIBES ALONG THE DANUBE, TO THE NORTH OF HIS
KINGDOM, AND THESE WERE NOW MORE OR LESS SUBDUED. THE CITY-
STATES TO THE SOUTH, HOWEVER, WERE STILL A MATTER OF CONCERN.

PHILIP'S BIGGEST PROBLEM WAS THAT LEADING AN ARMY ON A
CAMPAIGN INTO ASIA MEANT THAT HE HAD TO LEAVE HIS KINGDOM IN
TRUSTWORTHY HANDS.

PHILIP II KNEW THAT HIS COURT WAS RIVEN BY AMBITIOUS MEN
AND WOMEN. EVEN WHILE HE WAS CAMPAIGNING ON THE BORDERS,
THE MACEDONIAN COURT FED ON RUMOUR AND COUNTER-RUMOUR,
GOSSIP AND JEALOUSY WHICH EMERGED FROM THE WOMEN'S
QUARTERS. IT MADE THE KING VERY UNEASY, DESPITE THE FACT THAT
SUCH WHISPERINGS WERE THE NORM IN THE MACEDONIAN COURT.
THIS BEHAVIOUR CAUSED PHILIP TO QUESTION INTO WHOSE HANDS
HE COULD ENTRUST THE SECURITY OF HIS KINGDOM.

Alexander was kicking his heels in exile in Illyria and Olympias was, no doubt, plotting to ensure that the latest queen did not usurp her son's place in the line of succession. It was a matter of some urgency as Cleopatra was pregnant.

The Greek city-states to the south of Macedonia were a constant threat. In Athens, the orator Demosthenes had often spoken publicly about the danger of ignoring the threat from the "barbarians" in the north. It would, he declared, be stupid to let Philip gain too much power.

Philip had a difficult decision to make before he made his move first on the city-states and then into Asia.

It was at this moment that Demaratus, an old and trusted family friend, came to Philip on a visit from Corinth.

According to Plutarch, Demaratus was in a sufficiently privileged position as to be able to speak freely to the king. After the formal civilities, Philip asked him, "What sort of agreement exists between the Greek city-states?"

Demaratus retorted: "You have good reason to ask about the harmony between them when you have filled your own house with so much discord and disorder."

Philip listened to Demaratus, who believed that his young son Alexander could be trusted with the reins of power while his father continued to fight against the city-states for a secure Macedonia. He suggested that he went personally as a messenger from Philip to his stubborn son. It was time to bring Alexander back from exile said Demaratus. Philip wholeheartedly agreed. Demaratus would be the best man to persuade the hot-headed and angry young man to return.

Demaratus travelled to see Alexander in his exile and persuaded him that his father needed him. Alexander returned and agreed to act as regent and protect his father's back in case of trouble at court or on the borders to the north.

Philip left his son with a small army and one of his older generals. Meanwhile, he went on a military expedition into Thrace. He was determined to challenge the city-states.

BLOODING THE CUB

In 340BC the Maedi tribe, located on the northern borders of Macedonia, took advantage of Philip's absence and the perception that a boy – Alexander – would be weak and uncertain, and erupted in rebellion. They were determined to break free from Macedonian rule. They believed that Alexander, still only a boy, would be unable to defend his father's kingdom.

They could not have been more foolish. Alexander consulted the old general left behind by his father and then, leading the army left in reserve for him, defeated the Maedi, captured their city and drove out their leaders. To consolidate the victory and to ensure that there was no further trouble, Alexander brought in citizens from Greece and settled them in the Maedian capital, which he renamed Alexandroupolis. It was a portent of things to come.

It was a military blooding for the boy who had already showed what he was made of. He could be depended on to assess a threat, to consult, plan carefully and then to act with speed. He was ruthless in the execution of a battle. He was only a boy, but already the soldiers of the Macedonian army were impressed.

Now that the borders of Macedonia were secure and Alexander had proved clearly that he could act decisively as regent, Philip began to look again to the East and to freeing the Greek cities under the rule of the Persian Empire on the other side of the Aegean Sea. Before he could make that move, Philip had to ensure that the mainland Greek city-states were not a potential threat.

BARBARIANS

Macedonia and its king were regarded by orators like Demosthenes as "barbarians". The Athenians considered that theirs was the only civilized way in which to live. Demosthenes ridiculed the Macedonian kingdom and fed the overweening pride of the Athenian "polis".

Yet the city-states had reason to be afraid. For Macedonia had an army that, under Philip, was becoming more and more of a threat to the soft and settled cities to the south.

Sparta, a city devoted to warfare and the creation of soldiers, was unwilling to join in league with Athens and Thebes. Sparta did not rely, as they did, on bands of mercenary soldiers to fight their wars for them. As the citizens of the other city-states argued and disputed, Philip increased the pressure.

The Persian Empire sent help to Perinthus when Philip attacked it. Philip acted with speed when an excuse came his way. The Locracians of Amphissa were accused of ploughing up land that was sacred to Apollo. It was a time when some men believed that the gods were active in their concerns for men – that they interfered in their affairs on one side or another and it did not do to insult the gods, as the Locracians had done.

The Amphictyonic Council appealed for help from Athens and then from Thebes. Both refused to help and so the Council turned to Philip and begged him to help them punish the tribe who had insulted Apollo.

There are those who say that Philip may have engineered the situation himself. He would use any means he could to get what he wanted. If diplomacy would secure his objective, he used it. If, by stirring up one city against another, he could remove a threat, he would do just that.

If a situation required war or bribery then he would not hesitate to fight or bribe. He turned any situation to his own advantage in the power struggle that was developing between Macedonia and the city-states.

Philip knew that he dare not begin his great dream of invading the Persian Empire without ensuring that Athens and Thebes were no longer a threat. The invitation to interfere in the religious dispute about the sacred land gave him the chance to move. The Council had expected him to march to relieve the city of Amphisa, but instead, he took his army to the ruined fort at Elatea. This gave him a commanding position on the main route to Boeotia.

This move put great pressure on the Thebans and when he offered them the chance to join with him in a joint attack on Athens, the Athenians were terrified. Demosthenes advised the citizens of Athens to send a delegation to Thebes to offer them mercenary reinforcements. He did all he could to rouse the anger and fear of Athenians against the Macedonians, whom he saw, rightly, as a threat to their democracy.

Demosthenes said: "Philip's rise was due to Athenian apathy more than to his own power. Philip believes that every move must be an advance, while we never seem to get hold of reality. Philip knows very well that, if he does not have control of Athens and democracy, we are still a threat to him. We, in Athens, are the main hope for those threatened by force."

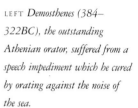

LEFT *Demosthenes (384– 322BC), the outstanding Athenian orator, suffered from a speech impediment which he cured by orating against the noise of the sea.*

BELOW *The ruins of Sparta, capital of the Greek state most opposed to King Philip II and Alexander the Great.*

Athens was inclined to look for a peaceful way out of the situation and Philip was patient. Then, in the summer of 338BC, he struck across the passes from Boeotia into Phocis and took Amphissa and from there his army surged down to the Gulf of Corinth and took Naupactus.

THE BATTLE OF CHAERONEA

This was the first set-piece battle in which Alexander was given a command by his father. He led the left wing of the cavalry and it was a defining moment in the young man's life. Plutarch wrote: "In our times an old oak tree was shown near the Cephisus, called Alexander's oak, because his tent had been pitched under it; and the piece of ground at no great distance, in which the Macedonians had buried their dead."

The allies, Thebes and Athens, were threatened by Philip's rapid move on their southern flank and abandoned the passes from Boeotia into Phocis and regrouped on the wide plain by the river at Chaeronea.

The armies waited. Thebes had a well-trained standing army, but Athens could only provide mercenaries, who were weak and untrustworthy – they were like corn before the scythe against the hardened Macedonians.

ABOVE *A marble statue of the Athenian orator, Demosthenes, who regarded the Macedonians as barbarians.*

Behind the Macedonian horde, the soft, rolling foothills rose from the wide, scrub-covered river valley. A few dark stands of pines broke up the sun-bleached land.

The allied armies of Thrace and Athens were restless. When would these Macedonians attack?

The order of battle for the allies had the Thebans on the right, the smaller allies in the centre and the Athenians on the left. Their numbers are not known.

Philip marched his army through the mountain passes of Boeotia and had come down onto his enemies at Chaeronea. It is thought that Philip possessed 30,000 infantry and 3,000 cavalry. He gave Alexander command of the left wing, facing the Thebans, while he confronted the Athenian mercenaries on the right wing. Philip's army approached the battlefield at great speed. The combined army of Thebes and Athens watched as their opponents arrived and waited for the Macedonian leader to make the first move. Philip was not going to be hurried. He knew the value of settling his men into their correct formations and of giving them time to recover from the speed of their advance.

The armies paused and took stock. Many would die in the plain on that bright day.

The Macedonian infantrymen, in their phalanxes, stood waiting. The soldiers held their spears levelled and bristling through the front rank of men. Those in the rear held their spears high until the moment came to move up and take the place of a dead comrade.

The Macedonian soldiers had spent many years learning their trade under Philip. They knew he expected nothing but victory and they were determined to give it to him. Despite their long and difficult march to the scene of the battle, they were calm and steady.

Alexander looked over the vast array of men before him. The sun glinting on spear points and plumed helmets. The rattle of armour and then the sudden silence before the men were committed into the rage of battle.

Beyond the field, in the trees along the river bank, carrion crows waited. They would have fat feasting before the day ended.

Many of the men under Alexander's command were not young, but they were a formidable fighting force. They would need to be, for their leader was young, eager and impatient to get into the roar of battle.

He looked along the line to where his father stood, quietly staring at the opposing force. Philip had already talked through the tactics of the first engagement with the leaders of each phalanx. Alexander and his cavalry knew exactly what they had to do. It relied both on split-second timing and absolute certainty when that moment came.

Philip was planning a dangerous and complex manoeuvre to draw the Athenians in the centre away from the protection of the right and left wings. This would expose the flanks of the enemy and there they were vulnerable to the speed and ferocity of a Macedonian attack. It was a gamble and a very hard manoeuvre to execute in the heat of battle, but Philip knew his men.

The sound of swords beating on shields rolled across from the opposite army. The Macedonians were silent, watching their king.

The Athenians were the first to make a move. Their inexperience showed as soon as they began to advance slowly towards Philip's infantrymen. Philip appeared to lose his nerve and began to falter. He ordered the phalanxes to give way. They moved backwards, just holding off the opposition with their long spears. The Athenian centre was drawn slowly further and further away from its defensive wings.

The Athenians scented an easy victory and began to charge. Even as the Athenians realized what was happening, Alexander threw himself and his cavalry into the gap between the Athenians and the "Sacred Band", the flower of the Theban army. After strong resistance, Alexander broke them and came through towards the centre.

Philip, meanwhile, had made a very difficult reverse. He ordered the phalanxes to go directly from retreat into steady attack. They moved inexorably into the Athenian centre where there was chaos caused by Alexander's attack on their wing.

BELOW *The great warrior Alexander (far left) fights King Darius of Persia (right) at the Battle of Issus.*

The Macedonian infantry broke through the Athenian lines and then wheeled left. At the same moment Alexander wheeled right and together they crushed the centre. The two wings were at the infantrymen's mercy and also at the mercy of the cavalry, who were already attacking the enemy flanks. The hacking, thrusting, smashing of metal blades into bone and flesh went on. Men and animals screamed in agony or roared in anticipation of victory. The allies from the city-states panicked and ran.

Demosthenes was one of the first to run from the field. "He did not hesitate to disgrace the inscription on his shield, on which was engraved in gold 'with good fortune'," wrote Plutarch.

Bold, fast and totally ruthless, this Macedonian army could inflict total destruction at will – another lesson Alexander learned from the Battle of Chaeronea.

Thebes and her allies suffered at Philip's hand. He was merciless to their soldiers and was delighted to see so many of their dead on the battlefield. He sold her captured soldiers into slavery, the leaders were banished or executed and the city was occupied by Macedonian soldiers.

In Athens, the citizens blamed Demosthenes and waited in fear of what Philip might do. They had already heard what he had done to the Thebans and to Thebes. They knew he was determined to begin his move into Asia and that he was capable of destroying anything that stood in his way.

But Philip had learned the lesson all colonizers need to know: the advantage of using a minority to rule the majority. With Theban power destroyed, he could afford to be magnanimous to Athens, the weaker party.

Philip wanted the goodwill of Athens and, to that end, he treated it well. In order to encourage Athens to become an ally, he sent the captured prisoners into the city. They were not ransomed, but set free. The Athenians were astonished at this gesture. Philip gave them even more.

Alexander and the general Parmenion carried the ashes of the dead who had fallen in the field into the city. Athens was won over to this generous victor. It left Philip without powerful enemies at home and meant that he could now advance into Asia without concerning himself about the enmity of the city-states.

Alexander would never forget the example of his father.

The Battle of Chaeronea was one of the decisive battles of ancient times, for with it came the end of the city-states as real powers. Philip was confirmed as the military leader of Greece. The Macedonians had come of age.

Philip created a new constitution and a council of representatives from each city. Corinth became the meeting place where all differences between the council members were to be settled. All members were responsible for keeping order within the Corinthian League and for defence against pirates, brigands and those wanting to upset the status quo.

Philip took the title of "hegemon" which was more acceptable than the title of "King" to the city-states. It meant that he could make unilateral decisions whenever he felt they were necessary.

PLOTS AT COURT

Meanwhile in the royal court at Pella, more intrigues were developing that would affect Alexander. Cleopatra had given birth to a girl and was pregnant again. Alexander's position as potential heir was becoming less and less secure.

Olympias was completely out of favour and Philip remembered only too well the strange portents he had seen when he had married her. She was also less important as a guarantee of his security in the north now that the tribes there had experienced the power of the Macedonian army.

Olympias still had friends in the court and they sent her news of the intrigues there. All around the Greek peninsula, from Halkidiki in the north to the Peloppenese in the south, there were small cities looking for ways to cement their alliances with Macedonia.

Pixodarus, satrap of Caria, saw an opportunity to create a military alliance with Philip. He had a daughter whom he offered to Philip's illegitimate son, Arrhidaeus. His mother was Philinna of Larissa. Arridaeus was simple-minded but that was no hindrance to the ambitions of Pixodarus. He sent an ambassador to negotiate the match.

Olympias heard about the plan, as did some of Alexander's closest friends. It was not long before Alexander heard a distorted account of the plan. What he heard suggested to him that his father was planning to settle the kingdom on Arrhidaeus after this marriage.

Alexander decided to act quickly and without discussion with his father. He knew how treacherous and dangerous the court in Pella could be.

He sent one of his friends, a tragic actor called Thessalus, to Caria to tell Pixodarus that Arrhidaeus was both illegitimate, and simple-minded. Thessalus suggested that Alexander would be a much better man with whom to forge an alliance. Pixodarus was delighted by the proposal.

When Philip discovered this intrigue he was furious. He sent for Philotas, son of Parmenion, the general and one of Alexander's close friends, and they went to Alexander's room.

In the scene that followed, Philip angrily demanded to know what Alexander thought he was doing. He had behaved badly by going behind his father's back and worse by offering to marry the daughter of a mere Carian. He was, after all, no more than the subject of a barbarian king. Was this the sort of woman Alexander wanted to marry?

Alexander was shamed by his father.

Philip ordered Thessalus to be brought back to Macedonia in chains and he also banished four of Alexander's closest friends.

These were Harpalus, who became controller of Alexander's treasury, Nearchus, who would be appointed Governor of Lycia and land as far as Mount Taurus, Erygius, who had command of the allied cavalry and Ptolemy, who became part of the king's bodyguard. They were exiled and Alexander was isolated yet again. They would only come back when Philip was dead.

Philip now made his first move to create a bridgehead into Asia. He sent Parmenion, his most experienced general, and another senior officer, Attalus, to reconnoitre the Hellespont and to create the means of crossing into Asia with an enormous army.

Alexander, in disgrace again, was forced to wait and take no part while his father forged ahead to realize his dream. Soon, there would indeed be nothing left for Alexander to conquer.

But Fate is a fickle thing and she was about to tip her scales in Alexander's direction.

CHAPTER THREE

ASSASSINATION
AND AMBITION

IN THE SPRING OF 336BC,
TWO SENIOR MACEDONIAN OFFICERS,
PARMENION AND ATTALUS,
WERE ORDERED BY PHILIP TO CROSS
INTO ASIA MINOR AT THE
HELLESPONT TO PREPARE A
BRIDGEHEAD FOR HIS PUSH
INTO ASIA.

IT WAS THE DAY AFTER THE WEDDING OF ALEXANDER'S SISTER, CLEOPATRA, TO THE MOLOSSIAN KING, ANOTHER ALEXANDER.

THERE HAD BEEN GREAT FEASTING THE PREVIOUS EVENING, YET, BY DAWN, THE THEATRE AT AEGEAE WAS FULL. SEATED ON THE CURVING STONE SEATS WERE LEADING FIGURES OF MACEDONIAN SOCIETY, AMBASSADORS AND DELEGATES FROM ALL OVER THE GREEK WORLD AND FROM THE TRIBES WHO HAD BEEN DEFEATED BY PHILIP AND HIS ARMY OVER THE YEARS.

THEY WERE EAGER FOR THE EVENTS OF THE DAY TO BEGIN. IT WAS TO BE A DAY OF DRAMA AND SINGING. A DAY OF CELEBRATION.

PHILIP WALKED IN THE PROCESSION BEHIND THE STATUES OF THE GODS. HE LIMPED SLIGHTLY. BESIDE HIM WERE HIS SON AND HEIR, ALEXANDER, AND THE BRIDEGROOM.

PROTECTING PHILIP AND CLUSTERED AROUND THE GROUP WERE HIS BODYGUARD AND TRUSTED FRIENDS. EVEN ON A DAY OF CELEBRATION, IT WAS NOT WISE TO RELAX SECURITY AROUND THE MIGHTY, ONE-EYED KING.

As they entered the theatre, Alexander looked up and saw the rows and rows of men and women looking down from the stone benches. He may have noticed a nondescript man holding the bridles of two horses standing in the dusty street outside the theatre in the shade of the high stone wall. The man looked away. The horses were saddled as if ready for a long journey. Alexander moved on with his father and the guards into the entrance to the orchestra.

The noise of the vast crowd hushed and stopped as the guardsmen stood aside to allow Philip to enter alone.

The guards' faces were grave. Each was armed with short sword and dagger.

Their eyes were never still. Some of them faced the crowded stone benches, others never took their eyes off their king.

Alexander may have felt a slight tug of concern. Why was there a man with two horses in the dusty street outside the theatre? Was his mother, Olympias, still angry with the king for putting her aside for a newer, younger woman? Something was wrong and it may have made him uneasy.

The guards took their places along the lowest wall of the theatre. They hardly glanced at the young prince as his father entered the theatre. They had a job and a duty to fulfil and they never forgot it. They had to protect the king.

Philip limped forward, looked up into the sun and the blue sky and blinked his seeing eye in the brightness. He lifted his hand in greeting and the gold buckle on his white cloak glinted in the sun. The crowd was silent.

Pausinias was one of the bodyguards. He had once had been Philip's lover, but had been cast aside, it seems, just as Philip cast aside his wives. But Philip was not cruel to old friends or lovers. Pausinias was one of the close inner circle and still one of those trusted as a personal bodyguard. However, he hated Philip. He felt slighted and ignored. No one listened to his complaints. Even Alexander had merely stared at him when he said he had been insulted by Attalus and the new bride, Cleopatra.

Alexander had murmured a line from Medea: "The father, bride and bridegroom all at once" and had then turned away. He was not going to get involved in a lover's tiff.

This indifference only heightened Pausinias's resentment. He was perhaps encouraged by Olympias, who wanted her son to replace his father.

She knew that Alexander's time was running out as Philip's favoured bride was nearing the end of her pregnancy. If Cleopatra gave birth to a son, Alexander's chances of succession would be limited. It may be that Olympias had promised Pausinias great rewards if he helped to achieve her ambition.

His hands sweating, Pausinias glanced around the line of bodyguards, motionless in the morning sun. Everything was in place. The people were waiting for their king to say the words, to make offerings to the gods and to open the proceedings on this joyful day.

Philip still stood, his arm raised. The royal ring was on his finger. Under the white cloak he wore a pale blue tunic. Simple, unadorned, as was right for a warrior king. He stood and looked slowly around the men and women and smiled a little. These were his conquests, these were his people.

The attack came fast. The only movement in the theatre. Pausinias raised his short sword to his waist and ran full at Philip. Before anyone could move, the blade entered below the ribcage of the king. He was dead before his body slid to the ground. Pausinias ran ... ran for the narrow corridor between the stone benches and raced for the half circle of light at the end of it. He was not fast enough. While most of the guards ran in horror to their king, three threw themselves across the flagged floor of the theatre to the opening into the streets.

Already the men and women in the theatre were on their feet. They were too shocked to make a sound. Pausinias, the assassin, panting, stood facing the three bodyguards and waited.

Already a companion had taken the white cloak and laid it over the face of his king. The three advanced on Pausinias without a word. They slaughtered him like a dog. A sword to the throat, another to his guts and, as he fell, another to his head. It was done. Pausinias was silenced.

On the floor of the theatre the blood of Philip was already beginning to dry in the morning sun. Alexander looked down at his father for a moment and then whirled and strode past the dead assassin, out of the theatre and into the street.

The two horses still stood there. Alone.

From this moment in 336BC, Alexander never stopped planning, moving on and fighting battles. From this moment until June 323BC, Alexander was driven by his ambition.

Proclaimed king by acclamation of the army at the moment of his father's death, the assassin already silenced, Alexander lost no time in securing his position. Amyantas, potential heir to the throne, was murdered.

Cleopatra, Philip's wife, was murdered by Olympias with her daughter. She had them both roasted alive. Her savagery was a warning of the ruthless ambition she had for her son. Alexander claimed to be appalled by the murders, and then had male members of Cleopatra's family slaughtered to prevent any problems with them in the future. Alexander was 20 years old.

There was, in short, a bloodletting. This was not unusual at the time. It could be claimed that the political killings were as much for the security of the kingdom as for the safety of the new king.

Alexander brought back his friends who had been sent into exile by Philip and, with his dearest friend, Hephaestion, they formed a tightknit band of young and ambitious men.

HEPHAESTION

The relationship between Alexander and Hephaestion may well have been sexual. Between young men such a relationship carried no social stigma. Indeed, at the time, such relationships were encouraged between warriors. The Spartans, for example, were said to place lovers together in the line of battle on the basis that they would not only fight for Sparta, but also for their partner.

It is certainly true that Alexander saw in his relationship with Hephaestion a reflection of the relationship between Achilles and Patroclus as told by Homer in the *Iliad*.

Greece and the city-states were delirious at the news of the death of Philip. They were determined that Alexander would be removed as hegemon of all Greece. Athens, in particular, was encouraged in this by the speeches of Demosthenes, who was told the news of Philip's death by secret messenger.

Demosthenes was in contact with Attalus, uncle of the murdered Cleopatra. He was now with the advanced guard of the army in Asia Minor. Demosthenes urged him to encourage his troops to rebel against Alexander.

Alexander received news of the treacherous messages passing between the Athenian and Attalus. He ordered Attalus' father-in-law, Parmenion, his most experienced general, to execute the traitor. Parmenion did not hesitate to do so.

RIGHT *Mountain villages, like this one in Northern Greece, were easy to defend. This meant that Alexander and his troops had to rethink their tactics if they wanted to have a fair chance of overpowering the villages on the mountain borders of the Macedonian Empire.*

SECURITY IN THE NORTH

At this delicately balanced time, Alexander was advised by older and more experienced men to treat the rebellions in the north with a moderating hand.

Having been defeated by Philip and promised new leadership, the tribes were still leaderless. They longed to have back their old tribal chiefs.

Alexander had to act quickly to rebuild his authority over the tribes along the river Danube.

The old chiefs, like Glaucis and Cleitus, believed it would be an easy matter to seize back their power from an untried youth like Alexander. Particularly as he was also without his most experienced general, who was at the Hellespont with an advance guard. Alexander was also threatened by the city-states in the south, which had the promise of help from the Persian Empire. It was a good time to revolt.

Alexander knew that taking the soft way with these tribes would be pointless. He would act firmly and decisively and impose his authority. If that meant war, then Alexander was not afraid to take that path.

ABOVE *The barren high ground in the Macedonian borders which was defended by a tribe called the Triballians.*

Warfare in the mountainous borders was unlike the traditional and formal pattern of warfare in the south. Fighting in the north depended on using guerilla tactics – it was a style of war that suited the quick-thinking and the resolute. It was a perfect battleground for a general of such imaginative and uncanny tactical perception as Alexander.

He was a natural general and tactician, not only in the set pieces of the battles he had already fought, but also in the fluid manipulation of rapidly shifting threats in harsh terrain.

A perfect example of Alexander's skill for sizing up a threatening situation and then reacting to it to his own advantage was when a tribe known as the Triballians held a strategic pass through which the Macedonian army had to advance.

The steep track was narrow and led up over the mountains where the Triballians held the heights. There they had massed heavy wagons and boulders.

As the Macedonian army marched up the track, towards the pass, they would let loose the wagons and the Macedonian army would be flung from the track into the gorge far below.

Alexander had to advance or all was lost. He dared not retreat. His outriders gave him warning of what faced them as they climbed the steep track. Alexander gave a simple order.

As the wagons were released from the top of the high pass the front ranks were to lie down and lock shields over their prone bodies. Most of the wagons would themselves fly over the prone men and into the gorge. The rest of the advancing Macedonians were to open ranks to let the wagons pass through them harmlessly. The discipline and the timing had to be exactly right.

The Triballians let loose their battering wagons; the front ranks of the Macedonians locked shields and lay down. The wagons flew over their prone bodies and mostly flew harmlessly into the gorge. Behind them the phalanx moved into open order and the remaining wagons passed between the ranks of soldiers. The instant the wagons had passed by, the Macedonian army formed ranks and charged the enemy, who ran.

On another occasion, Glaucias and Cleitus, the Illyrian leaders, surrounded Alexander's troops and all seemed lost. At that time, Alexander had an army of 12,000 men. Directly in front of the rebelling tribe's army he ordered his men to go coolly through their formal drill movements, doubling and turning, trotting and stopping without a word of command. It was a powerful display of absolute discipline and the Illyrian enemy fled in the face of it.

It was in this way that Alexander began to forge an army able to fight in set-piece battles with cavalry and archers, pike men and siege towers. Conversely, with its flying columns of lightly armed troops, they could take to the hills, live off the land and fight across desolate valleys and mountains, never knowing where the enemy might appear. They were, however, always ready for them.

Alexander was already a leader without fear and, while still an impatient young man, he was able to understand what the enemy would respond to and what would lead his armies to victory. Alexander showed evidence of being a great general. His men loved him for it. Would he also be a great ruler of men and conquered peoples? Time would tell.

THE THREAT FROM
THE CITY-STATES

Alexander must have felt frustrated, for he was not able to proceed to the next phase of his plan. Unless the restless ambitions and hopes of the people he would leave behind were resolved, he dared not set off for Asia.

The city-states were in a state of high excitement. Alexander knew that they had to be brought to heel. They believed that while he was busy fighting in the north they could regroup and regain their freedom from Macedonian rule.

Parmenion had advised Alexander to secure the borders along the Danube and said: "If I were you I would let the city-states go. Do not punish them."

Alexander replied, "Yes I know. If you were Alexander, that is what you would do. That is why you are Parmenion and I am Alexander."

He headed south. If necessary he would visit the wrath of a confident military and political leader on the rebellious cities.

Alexander marched fast to Thessaly where the Thessalians guarded the narrow pass that led to Thebes. He and his army had made a forced march of about 200 miles (322 kilometres) in six days. They had to get past the guarded high pass.

BELOW *Alexander meets the philosopher Diogenes who lived in a barrel. When Alexander politely asked if there was anything he could do for Diogenes, who was sunbathing at the time, he was told, "Yes, you can get out of my light."*

RIGHT *The magnificent Alexander the Great rides to meet King Porus of India wearing his signature white-plumed helmet. Painted by Charles le Brun (1619–1690) in 1673.*

The river Danube was bordered by steep, rocky slopes and trees which made the passage of an army very dangerous. The men would be forced into single file along the track and could be easily picked off.

Alexander talked to his engineers and instead of attacking the Thessalian guards who held the dangerous track along the edge of the river he had his engineers cut steps along and over the face of the mountain. In this way the Macedonian army bypassed the Thessalian army guarding the pass and effectively took Thessaly at a stroke.

He gained not only that victory but also the admiration and loyalty of the Thessalian cavalry. These cavalry regiments were to form a major part of his army in Persia and beyond. Soldiers love a victorious leader – they follow a lucky one.

Following this victory, the other city-states, who had banded together in the Corinthian League, backed down very quickly. Even Thebes agreed to Alexander's demands. The League confirmed Alexander as Philip's legitimate successor.

DIOGENES

At this meeting of the city-states, in Corinth, Alexander said he wanted to meet Diogenes, the philosopher who had abandoned all material things and lived in a barrel. He calmly refused to go and meet Alexander. If Alexander wanted to see him, then Alexander would have to come to him.

When Alexander went to meet Diogenes the eccentric old man was sunbathing. To everyone's horror he refused to stand up for his eminent visitor.

Alexander, amused perhaps by this stubborn old man, asked, "Is there anything I can do for you?" The old man bluntly replied, "Yes, you can get out of my light."

Alexander's companions were shocked at the philosopher's rudeness to their great leader. They were even more shocked when Alexander told them that if he were not Alexander he would like to be Diogenes.

ALEXANDER AND THE ORACLE AT DELPHI

ABOVE *The Amphitheatre at Delphi. Alexander's consultation with the Oracle at Delphi did not go as well as he had planned.*

Alexander was a religious man and, unusually for his time, he also respected the religions of other people. He took time to go to Delphi to consult the Oracle about his planned expedition against the Persians.

He arrived at the shrine at Delphi and found it shut. Alexander sent for the priestess, who refused to give him any reply to his questions. He asked her again and again, but she refused to make prophesy.

"I am forbidden by the law to make prophesy on such inauspicious days. Come another time," she said.

Alexander was not pleased and he tried to drag her by force into the shrine. As he dragged her there she cried, "You are invincible, my son!" and with that he let her go. "That is all the prophesy I want to hear," he said.

REVOLT AGAIN

Alexander turned to consolidate the victories he had had over the northern tribes and it was at this time that Demosthenes, in Athens, heard that Alexander had been killed in the battles in the north.

At the same time, the Persians were using bribery to gain the support of the Greek cities against the threat from Macedonia.

The peace that Alexander thought he had achieved amongst the city-states was in tatters once more. The Macedonian garrison he had left behind in Thebes was attacked. It was time for decisive action.

Within two weeks Alexander's army appeared outside the city of Thebes. To the consternation of the Thebans, the white-plumed helmet of Alexander could be seen amongst his men. He had marched an army – consisting of 30,000 men and 3,000 cavalry – 300 miles (483 kilometres) in just two weeks.

The Thebans refused to capitulate. They looked for help from Athens or Persia. The Athenians sent no help. Their other allies offered to send soldiers, but none arrived.

The omens were disastrous. The statues in the market place were said to have been seen sweating. And the waters by the city ran blood red.

The Thebans knew they could expect no quarter from Alexander. Their slaves, and even strangers in the city, were drafted to protect the walls, while the main Theban phalanx massed on the flat land beyond.

Alexander deployed one phalanx, his siege towers and catapults as well as other siege machinery against the newly built walls of the city. In the temples, the wives of the Theban soldiers prayed to the gods for help.

The Macedonians eventually broke through the Theban army and into the city. In frenzied terror the Theban soldiers rushed to save their women and children. It was a bitter and desperate business. Hand-to-hand, face-to-face, body-to-body they fought. Hard, disciplined and without pity.

Spears and sling stones were soon useless in the close-quarter fighting. The result was carnage. Blood stained the streets and ran along the gutters, men, women and children were viciously slaughtered by the pitiless warriors. "Every corner of the city was piled high with corpses," wrote Diodorus.

It had taken Alexander three months to take Thebes. He was angered by the delay, but worse, he was infuriated by the deaths of the Macedonian soldiers he had left behind in the city. It was sacked and looted and Alexander sold 20,000 of its citizens into public slavery. It was a terrible warning to any other disaffected people.

Even as this terrible, unremitting massacre went on, however, Alexander was able to show he could be more than generous. There were some citizens of Thebes who had been friends to Macedonia. He spared the descendants of the poet Pindar and ordered that his house be left alone. He also spared those whom he knew had opposed the revolt.

BELOW *Siege towers and siege weapons were used by the Macedonian army to destroy the city walls of Thebes.*

His treatment of Timocleia, a brave woman, illustrates Alexander's generosity best. Plutarch tells the story:

> "The calamities that that wretched city suffered were various and horrible. A party of Thracians demolished the house of Timocleia. The soldiers carried off the booty and the captain, having violated her, asked whether she had not some gold and silver concealed. She said she had and, taking him alone into the garden, showed him the well, into which she told him she had thrown everything of value when the city was taken.
>
> The officer stooped down to examine the well upon which she pushed him in and then dispatched him with stones.
>
> The other soldiers came back and found what she had done. They tied her hands and took her to Alexander.
>
> Alexander saw from the pride with which she walked in front of that savage crew that she was a woman of great spirit. He asked her who she was.
>
> She replied, 'I am the sister of Theagenes who was general of our army and fought against your father, Philip, for the liberty of Greece and fell at Chaeronea.'"

Alexander admired Theagenes' sister Timocleia not only for what she said, but for what she had done. He ordered that she be freed and brought to her children and that they should be allowed to leave the city unmolested.

Athens was another matter. According to Arrian, the news of the Theban disaster reached the city with the arrival of Theban refugees. The Athenians were in the middle of the celebration of the Great Mysteries, one of their most important religious festivals. The shock of the news that Thebes had been razed to the ground stopped the ceremony and the people of Athens began to haul all moveable property into the city from their farms in the surrounding countryside.

Panic set in. How were they to placate this king they had turned against? How to persuade him that their support for Thebes was only the result of a few foolish men who had roused the people?

Ten men were chosen by the Assembly because they were known to be friends of Alexander. They were to go and assure him that the Athenian people rejoiced at his victories in the north and that they approved of his punishment of the Thebans. It was all they could do – they had to pray that he would listen to them.

Alexander had calculated that he needed the Athenians on his side if he was to feel secure when he left for the Persian Empire. He told them he wanted the surrender of various troublesome men, including Demosthenes. Alexander reminded the Athenians that these men had encouraged the Thebans in their rebellion and were, therefore, as responsible as the Thebans themselves.

The Athenians, to their credit, asked him for mercy. Perhaps because he was in a hurry to get on with his ambitious plans, he agreed. Maybe it was because he remembered how his father had dealt with Athens when he had first threatened the city.

A few of the men Alexander had listed went into exile. One indeed, Charidemus, went to the court of Darius in Persia. Athens was surprised and relieved at the magnanimity Alexander showed at this time. But this was a lesson he had learned from Aristotle. Respect your enemy and be aware that one day you may need their help. He was beginning to grow as a diplomat as well as a military leader.

FINANCES

Alexander had an army, he had experienced generals, he had the dream. Now all he had to find was money. His army numbered 30,000 infantry and 4,000 cavalry at the lowest estimate and 43,000 infantry and 4,000 cavalry at the highest.

The cavalry was almost equally divided between Thessalian and Macedonian men and the other Greek states provided about 7,000 infantry and 600 cavalry.

All of these men and horses had to be fed, equipped and their families had to be provided for. Alexander was in debt, very much in debt. As much as 200 talents in debt.

Even with this debt, he would not begin the campaign until he had ensured that his friends and companions were financially secure. He gave away an estate to one, a village to another, or the revenues of some port or community to a third. By the time he had signed away almost all the crown property, a companion, Perdiccas, asked him, "Your majesty, what are you leaving for yourself?"

"My hopes," replied Alexander.

"Very well, then," answered Perdiccas. "Those who serve with you will share those, too." Perdiccas refused the gift he had been offered and several of Alexander's other friends did the same.

To ensure the safety of his supply lines and the peace of his borders, Alexander left Antipater, an experienced old soldier, in charge of a contingent of soldiers. Antipater had served under Philip as a trusted and expert military advisor and leader. It was essential for Alexander to be sure that Macedonia was in safe hands while he began an enterprise that would keep him away from his home for the rest of his life. Antipater was such a man.

Although Antipater was much older than his king, he served him loyally in Macedonia. It was Antipater who brought a halt to any intrigues and subdued any insurrection from the Northern mountain tribes. He even led a small army in victory over Sparta, and Alexander could be assured that Macedoina was secure under his leadership.

Alexander claimed he was only going to release the Greek settled cities on the coast of Anatolia, from Persian subjugation. This may have been the total of Philip's ambition and he may have stuck to it as an aim to ensure that his soldiers would come with him. Alexander, however, had greater dreams and bigger ambitions.

It was in this spirit that he led his army to the Hellespont on the road into Asia and beyond.

It was 334BC and the spring season for campaigns had come again. Alexander made an offering to Zeus, held games in honour of the Muses and Olympian games in Aegae.

A statue of Orpheus in Pieria was seen sweating. According to Plutarch, one seer told Alexander it was a sign that "Alexander would be written about in songs and epics, that poets would break sweat to create in celebrating his achievements."

Beyond the flat lands leading to the narrow waters dividing Europe from Asia, Alexander advanced. Behind him he left a kingdom in the safe hands of Antipater and sufficient men to protect the borders of Macedonia. To his north the mountain range, beyond the flat plain, to his south, beyond Halkidiki and the three fingers of land that spiked out into the Aegean Sea, lay Athens, Thebes and Sparta. City-states which would always be a thorn in his flesh, but for now they were quiet.

CHAPTER FOUR

A SPEAR
IN THE EARTH

4

ALEXANDER WAS NOW 22 YEARS OLD.
AT THE AGE OF 16, HE HAD TAKEN THE
THRONE BY ACCLAMATION, HE
HAD BEEN BLOODED IN BATTLE AT
CHAERONEA AND THEBES
AND, BY A SERIES OF JUDICIOUS
MURDERS, HE HAD SECURED
HIS POSITION AS KING.

ALEXANDER WAS NATURALLY AUDACIOUS AND MUCH OLDER THAN HIS YEARS. HE HAD AN INTUITION ABOUT WHAT DECISION WAS RIGHT OR WRONG, ABOUT THE PEOPLE HE TRUSTED AND ABOUT THOSE HE SHOULD NOT.

ALREADY HE WAS SHOWING THAT HE WAS MORE THAN THE MERE SON OF A POWERFUL FATHER, HE WAS A LEADER OF MEN. AND MOST OF THE 30,000 TO 45,000 SOLDIERS IN HIS ARMY WOULD WILLINGLY FOLLOW HIM WHEREVER HE ASKED THEM TO GO. AND, AS IT HAPPENED, HE ASKED THEM TO GO TO THE VERY END OF THEIR KNOWN WORLD.

EAGER FOR ACTION, YET CAUTIOUS IN TAKING IT, ALEXANDER KNEW THE VALUE OF LISTENING TO LOCAL KNOWLEDGE. HE PLANNED AHEAD AND TRIED TO ENSURE THAT HE AND HIS OFFICERS KNEW THE LIE OF THE LAND THAT THEY WOULD BE MARCHING AND FIGHTING OVER.

ALEXANDER WAS FEARLESS AND SEEMED TO UNDERSTAND MILITARY TACTICS INSTINCTIVELY. HIS MEN WERE CONFIDENT IN HIS LEADERSHIP BECAUSE HE WAS, ABOVE ALL ELSE, CONFIDENT IN HIMSELF AND THE ABILITIES OF HIS MEN. THIS TRUST FUELLED HIS AMBITION AND MADE POSSIBLE WHAT WAS TO COME.

CHARACTER

Son of a strong-minded and determined father. Son of a devious, ruthless and worldly-wise mother. Alexander could so easily have been a powerful and despotic leader yet, because of his liberal education under Aristotle, he was open-minded and inquisitive. He was unprejudiced, generous, merciful and fair. He possessed his mother's cunning and his father's confidence.

Plutarch, writing many years after the events, but using sources as near as contemporary to Alexander as possible, wrote about the character of the man: "On his days of leisure, as soon as he was risen, he sacrificed to the gods; after which he ate. The rest of the day he spent in hunting, or deciding the differences among his troops or in reading and writing."

The daily life of a Macedonian king was a round of hearing grievances, offering help, making judgements and providing justice for the men and women who came to him and asked for it. And, when he had a chance, he would read, as Aristotle had advised him. This, though, was not the life he dreamed of.

Plutarch went on: "If he was on a march which did not require haste, he would exercise himself in shooting and throwing the javelin, or in mounting and alighting from a chariot at full speed. Sometimes also he diverted himself with fowling or hunting. All military skills delighted him and he was expert with all weapons."

Here is the picture of an ambitious but well-ordered man. A man looking for perfection in what he did. Yet he was also a man who took seriously the need to consider others:

> "On his return to his quarters, when he went to be refreshed with
> the bath and with oil, he enquired of the stewards of his kitchen
> whether they had prepared everything in a handsome manner for

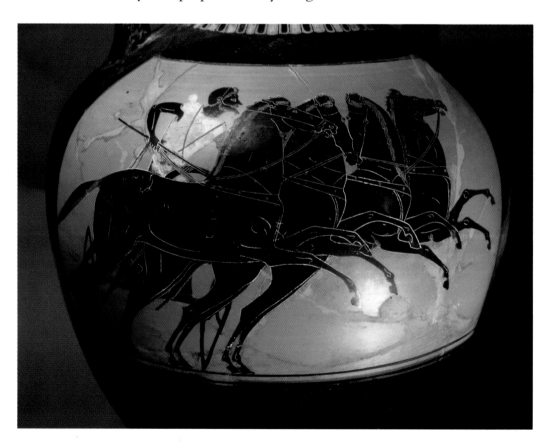

supper. It was not till late in the evening, and when night was come on, that he took this meal. He was very attentive to his guests at table, that they might be served equally and none neglected. His entertainments lasted many hours, but they were lengthened out rather by conversation than drinking."

Then Plutarch hints for the first time that Alexander would sit for a long time over his wine. Plutarch assured his readers that it was "for conversation's sake". There are others, however, who suggest that if he had any weakness it was for too much unwatered wine. There were certainly events later in the campaign when he acted with drunken folly and not as a result of carefully considered decisions.

Plutarch, however, would have it otherwise. For the moment Alexander was about to bring life to his dream. What was the nature of the adventure Alexander had taken on?

THE PERSIAN EMPIRE

Founded by Cyrus the Great, the Persian Empire was a vast focus of power. By the time Alexander had made the decision to expand his father's dream and to conquer the huge empire, it stretched from the Caucasus to the Mediterranean as far as Egypt and from the Indus Valley to the borders of Ethiopia. The Persians had managed to impose a relatively peaceful rule throughout their vast empire.

Compared with the cruel and tyrannical regimes imposed by the Assyrians and the Babylonians, the Persians were relatively tolerant of the customs and habits of the peoples of their empire. Unusually, they even gave respect to the local gods and people under their control responded well to their rule. Provided the conquered people submitted to being ruled by a Persian nobleman (a satrap) and provided that they paid the taxes demanded by the king, things were reasonably benign. The Persians had understood that most people, even the vanquished, want peace and quiet and the chance just to get on with their lives. They did not want any more trouble so long as they had food and land and some measure of freedom.

The Persian rulers, however, relied on mercenaries to provide the backbone of their armies. This left them time to enjoy a Sybaritic lifestyle in the royal courts which according to some made them soft and pampered. It certainly did not prepare them for what they were about to confront.

Alexander claimed that he came to avenge the excesses of Xerxes who had taken the Greek settlements along the coast of Asia Minor. There is no doubt that this was merely an excuse for him to take the settlements as his own, yet Alexander swore this as his aim to the rulers of Athens, Thebes and Sparta. It would be hard for them to rebel against the Macedonian plans if this was the true reason for the expedition.

The truth was that Alexander had his mind on greater and wider matters. Once he realized that conquest and rule did not necessarily mean heavy-handed military dictatorship, he was freed of the need to constantly hold down the people he left behind with large military contingents as he continued his march.

Leaving the people he conquered relatively free was a lesson well learned. When he at last decided to make the move on the Persian Empire, this made possible the miracle of his army's long and difficult advance into Persia towards Persepolis. He planted garrisons near major cities, but often he left the original ruler in place to ensure a safe transition and to leave him free to march on.

There were, however, difficult and dangerous matters to attend to before Alexander and his army turned inland to confront Darius.

Parmenion had already faced the military might of the Persian army when he was preparing the landing ground beyond the Hellespont, for Philip, Alexander's father. At that time Parmenion was faced with an army led by Memnon, who had 20,000 Greek mercenaries at his disposal and Parmenion was pushed back to his defensive lines. A stalemate developed.

Memnon had a problem. He came from Rhodes and, though he was a great and respected general, he was not Persian. The Persian commanders were jealous of both his skill and the popularity he commanded with the soldiers.

Memnon had devised a plan to defeat the Macedonian invaders that was ruthless and that might have been devastating, had he been allowed to follow it through. He argued with the Persian king and generals that when the Macedonian army invaded they should be not be engaged in a full-scale battle. They should be gradually sucked into the vastness of the landmass. Meanwhile, using the vastly superior Persian navy, he would put pressure on the Greek city-states to rise against the Macedonians on the mainland.

At the same time, he would adopt a scorched-earth policy so that Alexander had no supplies from the land. Memnon would then cut Alexander's supply lines from the coast and so isolate the invaders and pick them off at will. Simple and effective, it is a tactic that has worked successfully for generals throughout history: Napoleon retreated from Moscow through a terrible winter; Hitler's army retreated across the scorched earth from Stalingrad ... Overstretched lines of communication result, very often, in defeat for an invader.

The problem for Memnon was that the local leaders (satraps), who were Persian, refused to allow any of their villages to be burned. Their pride made them think that they could easily force this foreign army from their empire and they were certainly not prepared to listen to the ideas of Memnon from Rhodes. By the time they realized they were wrong, it was too late.

Alexander had more than his share of good fortune.

The Persian satraps were deluding themselves. It may even have been that Darius did not take the threat too seriously. He left the command of the army to Memnon when the moment for that first confrontation came. It was a serious error to have forced the Persian leaders to listen to Memnon and to act on his advice

THE PERSIAN NAVY

This was a force of some 400 ships which had control of much of the Aegean Sea. It was resupplied from the cities down the coast from Troy to Halicarnassus. The ships, manned to a large extent by sailors from Crete, Cyprus or Rhodes, were a threat to the rear of Alexander's proposed line of invasion. His supply lines were vulnerable and the Persian navy had a history of traffic into the Greek mainland through the islands off Greece.

It was this knowledge that would dictate Alexander's next line of march. After fighting at the river Granicus, he would head directly south and secure the hinterland of those ports so that he could strangle the Persian naval supply lines.

It would only be when he had neutralized, in part, this powerful arm of the Persian military that he would himself abandon his own ships and take the crews into his army.

The Persian navy was composed mainly of powerful triremes. These were manned by three banks of oarsmen. They had a central mast and were reinforced in the prow with a long battering ram that curved below the waterline. It was a terrible weapon in close combat. The ships also carried archers and some soldiers for hand-to-hand fighting. Their primary weakness was that they continually needed to find supplies of fresh water and food. Deny the oarsmen water and these ships were rendered practically useless.

INSET *A full-size, sea-going replica of a Persian trireme.*

DARIUS

Maybe Darius had been seduced by the soft life he led. Once he had been a fine general, but since being made king, Darius enjoyed the sumptuous life of the Persian court. The food and clothes, the customs and the rituals were all designed to reflect a belief that the Persian Empire could not be threatened. Darius had come to the throne in 336BC. He had been placed there by a kingmaker called Bagoas, a eunuch who had already arranged for the murder of his two predecessors.

Darius was respected and a hero, famous for his bravery in battle and in single combat. He had consolidated his position as king by crushing revolts as far afield as Egypt and his northern borders towards Afghanistan. He began to feel the need to be independent from the ruthless Bagoas, who, in turn, could feel his power over Darius slipping. He tried to murder Darius, but, forewarned, Darius made Bagoas drink the poison from the goblet that the eunuch had prepared for him.

The Persian Empire was rapidly sliding into decadence. The king and his nobles believed that Persian rule could not be toppled by an invading army from the mountains of Macedonia. How could anyone believe that an army, led by a young and inexperienced man, whose position relied on the loyalty his army had for his father, Philip, could defeat the might of the Persian Empire?

This was a dangerous misreading of the ambition, the personality and the skills of Alexander. A ruthless, young and inventive general, he commanded an experienced and hungry army which would cut the vast armies of Persia to shreds. Alexander also had one asset worth almost everything to a general ... luck. His men sensed it and rode his luck with him.

Alexander came down into Asia like the wrath of a god. If, as he claimed, he was the descendant of Achilles, then he was also descended from the gods. Thetis, the mother of Achilles, was a goddess of the sea.

THE ADVANCE

Who did Alexander take with him across the Hellespont?

He planned to take half the Macedonian infantry, two-thirds of his cavalry and other light-armed infantry. It left few men to hold down Macedonia or to protect it against outside threats from the northern borders or from the Greek city-states in the south.

Alexander also planned to take 22 triremes and 38 smaller warships and their crews of 6,000 men from Halkidiki. The Greek city-states had agreed to supply some infantry and cavalry as well as more ships. Thirty thousand men were to march into Asia with the young general at their head.

THE LEGEND OF THETIS AND ACHILLES

Achilles' father was Peleus, a mortal, and his mother was Thetis the sea goddess. Thetis knew that if she bathed her child in the waters of the river Styx, which mortals cross when they die, he would be safe from earthly harm. She took her baby, held him by his heel over the dark, raging waters and dipped him into the cold river.

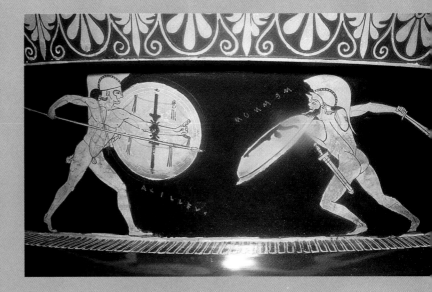

And the time came when Achilles was grown into a great warrior that he fought Memnon, a champion of Troy, and killed him. But it was a chance for the sly Paris watching from the walls of Troy. As Achilles raised his hand in triumph and turned his back on Troy, Paris let fly an arrow. It flew as a hawk flies to make its kill – remorseless, eager, unchangeable. It flew straight and true and found the only place Thetis had not protected. It smashed through Achilles' heel, by which Thetis had dangled him in the waters of the Styx. The arrow killed him.

(*The Iliad* – retold by Nick McCarty, published by Kingfisher Books.)

There were also zoologists, botanists, geographers, astronomers and astrologers amongst the train that followed Alexander to war. Alexander had imbibed the lessons he had been taught by Aristotle and remained as curious about the places he was going to overrun as he was determined on victory.

It took only three weeks for the army to march from Pella to the Hellespont. They marched 20 miles (32 kilometres) each day, carrying weapons, food and all their equipment for war.

Arrian describes an incident: "On the twentieth day after his departure from Macedon he arrived at Sestos, from where he marched to Eleaus, where he sacrificed upon the tomb of Protesilaus because he of all Greeks who accompanied Agamemnon's army to the siege of Troy set his foot first on the Asiatic shore. The reason for the sacrifice was that on his descent into Asia he might be more successful than Protesilaus." Protesilaus was also one of the first to die.

Alexander sacrificed a bull as they crossed the water in an offering to Poseidon and then poured wine from a golden cup into the dark sea to appease the Nereids.

The ships came out of the early morning mist towards the landmass that was Asia and Alexander steered the first of them.

Arrian goes on to report: "Alexander, in his full armour, leapt down into the foaming waters and waded ashore, alone. He looked up into the morning sunshine and drove his stabbing spear into the land."

It was a sign, Alexander believed, that he had finally begun to fulfil his destiny. He was claiming Asia for his own. Shortly after arriving on land, Alexander left his army to disembark and set up camp and went, with a small party, to the city of Troy. There he built an altar and made a sacrifice to Athena, goddess of Troy. He then made a gift of his armour to the temple

INSET *Achilles, Alexander's hero, fights Memnon during the Trojan war. Achilles wields an ancient stabbing spear and Memnon a sword.*

BELOW *A stone relief portraying ancient sailors rowing a trireme – 400 BC.*

and, in exchange, helped himself to the weapons which hung on the walls. Some say that he had these weapons, which were relics of the Trojan war, carried before him in battle.

Alexander was a truly religious man, but he also knew what was at stake and covered all his options by offering a sacrifice to Priam, who had been King of Troy at the time of its defeat by the Greeks.

Arrian goes on to say: "His sailing master, Menoetius, crowned him with gold, as did Chares the Athenian, who came with Greeks and others. Alexander's close friend, Hephaestion, laid a wreath on the tomb of Achilles' dear friend, Patroclus, while Alexander laid one on the tomb of his ancestor, Achilles. Having done that he turned to his friend and remarked, 'How lucky Achilles was to have had Homer to proclaim his deeds and to preserve his memory.'" It is true, the only chronicler that Alexander had was a second-rate writer called Calisthenes.

The Persian army, under the command of Memnon, waited beyond the river known as Granicus. A scouting party sent forward by Alexander, and led by Hegelochus, scanned and

THE STORY OF PATROCLUS

Warriors at this time often fought in pairs. It was found that those who were lovers fought best together and the bonds of affection made them very nearly invincible. There was certainly no sense of there being anything morally wrong with such a deep friendship between men. The power of love is clear in this story about Achilles.

"When Patroclus died outside the gates of Troy, Achilles was driven to fight again. He vowed to avenge him. The body of Patroclus was brought to the Greek camp by Meriones and Menelaus.

They carried it through the roaring noise of battle and men stopped their bloody business as the body passed. For a moment it seemed as if the sun had gone out of the world.

Achilles then did things that he would never have done had he not been driven wild with grief at the death of his best friend. The body was placed on a pyre surrounded by herbs and dressed in white then around him they laid his weapons and armour. Achilles forced 20 Trojan captives onto the mighty pyre and burned them all. A sacrifice for his lover.

Then, the sun setting behind him, Achilles stood with his hair flying in the wind and smoke, looked out over the battlefield and called a challenge to the man who had killed his dear friend … And war began again."

(*The Iliad*, a retelling by Nick McCarty, published by Kingfisher Books.)

assessed the banks of the river and the land where the Persians had drawn up. Alexander wanted to know everything about his enemies. Their disposition, their composition, their choice of armour and weaponry, and the lie of the land before he committed his men to this first major battle of the campaign.

INSET *Achilles dresses the wound of his lover, Patroclus. From a Greek cup dated fifth-century BC.*

THE BATTLE AT THE RIVER GRANICUS

In the hours before dawn Alexander, Parmenion, Philotas, Parmenion's son who led the companions cavalry, Amyantas, who led the lancers, Calas, who led the Thessalian cavalry, Craterus, Meleager and Philip, who commanded the infantry battalions and Cleitus the Black, met for a situation report and tactical discussion. They sat outside Alexander's tent while all around them thousands of men slept alongside their spears and swords.

A few men stirred and moved about in the early morning light, gathering wood. Smoke from cooking fires drifted into the sky. But, apart from the occasional yelp of a dog and the restless movement amongst the horses, everything was still and quiet.

The leaders knew from the situation reports brought in by Hegelochus, who led the reconnaissance parties, that the enemy was drawn up to make a stand on the far bank of the river Granicus. It was not far away. It flowed from its source on Mount Ida and down to the Sea of Marmara.

The Granicus was in flood and the main body of the Persian cavalry was positioned in front of the Greek mercenary infantrymen.

When Alexander first heard this he was astonished. Why place the cavalry in a position where they were restricted? They could not move forward because of the river and the steep banks, they could not move backwards because behind them were ranged the ranks of the Greek mercenary infantrymen.

The Persians had clearly overruled Memnon and demanded that their cavalry had pride of place in the battlefield. The arrogance of the cavalry was to continue to be a problem through the ages – what is more, it would cost the Persians this first battle.

The council meeting was not easy. The leaders Alexander had to control were, for the most part, powerful and experienced men. They had campaigned with Alexander's father when Alexander was still a child. He was wise enough to appear to listen, at least.

"My lord," said Parmenion. "We shall advance to the river by mid-afternoon. Their infantry is out-numbered by ours according to the reports we have. They won't risk waiting so close to us through the night. So they will withdraw and we can get across easily at dawn."

Alexander nodded and even appeared to consider the idea for a moment.

"Yes, Parmenion? Go on."

"There is great risk in attacking as things are right now. The river is deep."

"Yes, we know. Hegelochus did a thorough check. We know the river is deep and that the banks are steep where their army is marshalled."

"Exactly, my lord. And we can't attack on a broad front and make use of our extra numbers. We would have to attack in columns, in very loose order and we would have their cavalry cutting us to shreds in a spit."

The old soldier had good reason for his concern. His sons, also at the council meeting, nodded in agreement.

"To face a possible defeat at this stage would be folly, my lord."

Alexander looked at the old, battle-scarred man. "Defeat, Parmenion? By this pissing little river? We crossed the Hellespont. It would blush for shame if we were stopped by this trickle of water. I, too, would be ashamed to be stopped by such a stream. We are fighting men and to hesitate now would be unworthy of us.

"The enemy would be encouraged to think they can beat us … They might even begin to think they were as good soldiers as we are."

He smiled around the group and his eyes caught theirs in the white light of the dawn. The commanders began to smile. His certainty was infectious. Arrian wrote of him: "He was very handsome in person and much devoted to exertion. He was active in mind and courageous and proud of his honour. He enjoyed danger. He was clever enough to know by instinct what had to be done while others were still dithering … He was skilled in rousing the courage of his men and, because he had no fear himself, others around him felt fearless, too. He acted with great boldness, even when he was not certain of the result."

This was the young man these veterans listened to on that morning in May in the flat river valley. He had decided.

"We advance, my friends. I will ride on the right wing. Parmenion will command the left and Philotas, you shall command the right. We know what we must do … Be sure your men know their business."

LEFT *The vicious hand-to-hand combat between the Macedonians and the Persians at the Battle of the Granicus.*

The sun rose over the low, scrub-covered hills. In the distance, the soft line of more blue hills lay under the pale, pearly sky of a perfect morning. On Alexander's right flank there was a lake which protected the flank if it could be held. The river was no little stream ... It had been fed by the spring waters from the mountains and was running strong.

Marked out by the white plumes on his silver helmet, Alexander sat on his magnificent horse and surveyed his army. Behind him rode his eight bodyguards, chosen for the honour because they were his friends. Hephaestion would certainly have been one of them. Cleitus another.

Before him the army was suddenly quiet. Waiting. This was a beginning for them, too. They

looked up at their young commander and felt a rush of confidence. He would lead them well they believed and that, for a general, is half the battle won.

Battles at this time were often the chance to settle personal vendettas. Hand-to-hand fighting was often the way battles developed. It was a bloody business. Sword against sword, spear against spear. Men looked each other in the eyes and hacked and stabbed, killed and killed again in a frenzy of blood, screams and chaos.

It was not unusual for particular heroes to look for their counterpart on the battlefield and to confront him in a duel to the death and it was usual for the main target of all soldiers to be the enemy general. Once he was killed, very often his side would break down and run for their lives.

So Alexander made himself a target in his silver helmet and white plumes. He was not afraid to be the main target of the enemy, for in that way he could distract their commanders from what was happening in the battlefield itself.

Intelligence reports had made it clear that the Persians were armed with light javelins and not the long lances the Macedonians favoured. Javelins were light for throwing, but were not very accurate if hurled from horseback.

Alexander's men were skilled shock troops. The infantrymen were armed with their 15-foot (four-and-a-half-metre) lances as well as swords and shields. When they advanced, all the enemy saw was a hedge of blades advancing, disciplined and steady as rocks.

For the moment the two armies waited. It was a moment of silence. The Persians drawn up in position on one side of the river. The horses' harnesses glistening in the sun. As Alexander made the final adjustments to his battle formation, the Persians could easily pick him out.

He marshalled his best cavalry force on the right. The Persians assumed that the attack would come to them onto the Persian left. Their assumption was wrong.

Alexander's army had a company of archers on its right flank ensuring there was no way to break through down the narrow flank between the army and the shores of a lake. His cavalry, under Parmenion, were all on the left flank. In the centre, the terrifying phalanxes of infantry soldiers waited. Tense. Thoughtful. They were facing death and they knew it.

Alexander looked across the river and knew this was a dangerous moment. If he failed and his army was defeated he would lose both his reputation and the admiration of his men. He would be harried back to his base on the coast and be forced to rethink the whole campaign. His adventure depended on convincing the Persians, and his own men, that he was unbeatable.

To this end he had devised a strategy of thrust and counter-thrust which, in the terrain he was attacking, was dangerous, very difficult and relied on great courage and discipline from his men. It also needed split-second timing if his waves of attack were not to become entangled with one another. But he commanded an army who understood what was demanded of them and who would deliver.

Like Achilles facing the Trojans, no doubt, Alexander felt that rush of excitement and then the cold and calculating certainty of his coming victory. He had no room for doubts.

A trumpet sounded ... men drummed with their spears on their shields. The river ran fast in front of the soldiers. The Granicus, in spate, could rip an unwary man off his feet and drown him under the weight of his armour and weapons. It could make holding a line difficult even without having to fend off the hail of light javelins launched from the high bank ahead of them. For the cavalry to charge into battle across the swirling waters was fraught with danger. Yet this is what was about to happen.

Trumpets sounded again. The battle that would be known as the Battle of the Granicus was about to begin. The men raised their battle cry to the god of war. Alexander moved his horse forward. His silver helmet, with its white plumes, gleamed in the May sunshine. Black carrion crows fluttered in the few trees that lined the banks of the river and waited.

LEFT *Crowned in his white-plumed helmet, Alexander leads his army through the raging current of the Granicus and into battle.*

CHAPTER FIVE

BLOOD
ON THE
EARTH

FOR A MOMENT THE MACEDONIAN AND PERSIAN ARMIES WERE STILL. THE PERSIANS WAITED FOR ALEXANDER'S ARMY TO STEP INTO THE SWIRLING RIVER GRANICUS AND CROSS UNDER THE STEEP BANKS INTO THE KILLING GROUND.

THE FIRST ATTACK CAME FROM THE MACEDONIANS. AT THE LAST MOMENT, ALEXANDER SWITCHED THE DIRECTION OF ATTACK SO THAT RATHER THAN APPROACHING FROM THE RIGHT, THE FIRST CAVALRY CAME DIAGONALLY INTO THE LEFT WING OF THE PERSIANS. THE PERSIAN CAVALRY HURLED JAVELINS INTO THE FIRST WAVE OF MACEDONIANS. A MACEDONIAN CAVALRY SECTION CHARGED ACROSS THE RAGING TORRENT TOWARDS THE PERSIANS HIGH ON THE BANK.

ALEXANDER LED THE CAVALRY ON THE MACEDONIAN RIGHT OBLIQUELY INTO THE WATER TO PREVENT A FLANK ATTACK ON HIS INFANTRY AS THEY CLIMBED OUT OF THE WATER ON A SOLID FRONT.

THE AXIS OF ALEXANDER'S ATTACK, THEREFORE, WAS ON TWO VERY CLOSE FRONTS WHICH SWITCHED DIRECTION AND THREATENED TO SWING THE PERSIAN LINE AND TO EXPOSE THEIR RIGHT FLANK TO ATTACK BY THE MACEDONIAN LEFT. LUCKILY, THE PERSIAN ARMY HAD VERY FEW IN RESERVE AFTER THEIR INITIAL ATTACK AND WERE MUCH MORE VULNERABLE.

A STRUGGLE NOW DEVELOPED TO GAIN A FOOTING ON THE FAR BANK.

Arrian wrote: "The trumpets sounded and the men raised a loud battle cry as he entered the water. Alexander kept his line oblique to the tearing current as the troops went over. He did this in case the enemy should attack before they drew up on the far shore. This way he made it possible to engage the enemy with a solid front … The banks were slippery with mud at first and once battle was joined even more so with blood. Javelins continued to fly down into the Macedonians struggling through the water towards a small shingle strip. Others though had struggled onto dry land."

Here was hand-to-hand fighting. Javelins flying, horses rearing and stamping, the long spears of the Macedonians were thrusting and stabbing as they slowly gained the foothold Alexander needed. Above them on the high banks, the Persian cavalry tried to stand firm. Memnon and his sons were in the thick of the battle.

Alexander rode in front, his horse streaming with the water of the Granicus. They charged into the mêlée. Alexander's white plumes marked him out for his enemies, just as he intended.

As his phalanx moved steadily into the attack, their long spears began to cause havoc with the enemy, who had no weapon to counter the 15-foot (four-and-a-half-metre) blades.

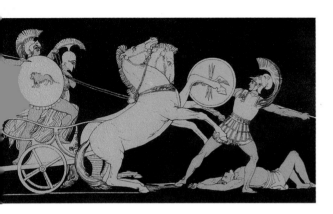

Alexander attacked and his spear was shattered. He turned and called to Aretis, one of his grooms, for another. Aretis was fighting a group of Persians and could offer no help. Alexander parried a Persian battle axe with the shaft of his spear. Aretis called through the din that he would have to ask someone else, at which Demaratus, a Corinthian and one of his bodyguards, gave him his spear.

At that moment Alexander saw Mithridates, Darius' son-in-law, riding with a squadron of his cavalry completely detached from the main body of Persians.

Alexander, ever reckless, charged in front of his men and slashed at Mithridates' face with

his spear. Mithridates fell to the ground with blood streaming from his wound. Rhesaces, a Persian, raised his curved sword and, aiming at Alexander's head, sliced off part of Alexander's helmet. Indeed the blade touched Alexander's hair. Alexander was onto Rhesaces in an instant and drove his spear through his enemy's breastplate.

Already Spithridates had driven his horse forward to attack Alexander from behind. He was close enough to lift his scimitar and swung at Alexander's unprotected back.

Cleitus the Black was too quick for him, however. He slashed down with his sword and sliced Spithridates' shoulder and sword arm from his body. He saved his friend Alexander's life.

All around the battle raged. The Macedonian infantry had now secured a foothold on the far bank of the Granicus and the Persians were backed into the faces of the Greek mercenaries who had been held in reserve. Flight was difficult, and, as the Macedonian infantry continued to advance, Alexander unleashed his lightly armed shock troops, who forced their way in amongst the panicking Persian cavalry.

The centre broke and now all the Macedonians had to do was to mop up the enemy troops. Alexander ordered them to concentrate their efforts on the Greek mercenaries who stood shoulder-to-shoulder on a hill.

At one point the Greeks offered to surrender – meaning they would have offered their services to their conqueror.

Plutarch records that Alexander, "in this instance allowing himself to be guided by passion rather than his reason, advanced in a charge against them and was so warmly received that he had his horse killed under him. It was not the famous Bucephalus which was killed by a sword in the ribs."

He refused the Greek mercenaries' offer and, apart from 2,000 who were taken prisoner, slaughtered the rest. It was a calculated act, unlike the generosity he usually showed to brave opponents. It seems that Alexander was determined to instil the fear of his army and of himself in whoever opposed him. Killing the Greek mercenaries so ruthlessly certainly sent out that message. The 2,000 he captured were sent to work as slaves in the mines in Macedonia. (Recently the remains of men from that time, chained together, have been found in the region.)

The figures given for those who died vary wildly, depending on whose account is believed. Plutarch says the Persians lost 25,000 infantry and 2,500 cavalry and that Alexander lost only 34 men. What is certainly true is that the Persians lost many of their best commanders in the battle and this affected the future conduct of the war.

It was at this moment that Alexander showed his true genius. He left the comfort of his tent and went down to the lines where his wounded lay. There were many who would die before the night was out, but all of them were anxious to tell their stories to their king. He encouraged them to boast of their bravery and skill, to talk, as soldiers always do, of those they had beaten and of those they had saved.

Here was a general who understood and cared for his battle-weary men and for the wounded and the dying. His actions may have been the result of the sweetness of victory, but he showed that he knew how much he relied on the ordinary fighting man and how much he valued them. His army rewarded him with their admiration and their gratitude. To him, it was an invaluable gift.

Alexander came away from his wounded soldiers and decreed that all his men who had died were to be buried with their arms and armour and that their parents and their children should no longer pay taxes on land or property.

All who had died in the battle, including the Greek mercenaries, who had caused such bloodshed amongst his own men, were given an honourable burial. The Persian officers were also buried with proper ceremony.

RIGHT *Athena, the goddess of Athens, dominates her temple on the Parthenon.*

Alexander had lost many of his closest friends in the battle. He declared that they were all heroes and, in memory of them, ordered the great sculptor, Lyssipus to create bronze statues of each of them. These statues were to be set up alongside the statues of kings. Alexander knew that the gesture of honouring these men would be popular both with the soldiers and in Macedonia and Greece.

Three hundred suits of finest Persian armour stripped from the dead in the field or from the enemy stores they had captured were sent to Athens to be dedicated to Athena on the Acropolis. It was by these gestures that Alexander fuelled his ambitious plans to draw in the loyalty of the Greek city-states. It also showed that he recognized the help their soldiers had given in the victory at Granicus.

THE RESULTS OF THIS VICTORY

Alexander divided up the spoils of the war and sent the gold and rich cloths that were his part of the booty, to his mother in Pella.

Then he turned to the serious business of securing his supply lines before he set off towards Cappadocia to the west and on through Mesopotamia, down into Assyria and across the Zagros Mountains to the Persian Gates leading to Persepolis and the conquest of Persia.

He could not march directly after the scattered remains of the army he had just smashed. They retreated into the

ABOVE *The spoils of war – a seventh-century BC bronze shield.*

Asian hinterland to regroup. Alexander knew he still had to destroy the power of the Persian navy in the Aegean and across the Mediterranean as far south as Egypt.

LEFT *Thracian silver jewellery of the fourth-century BC.*

THE LINE OF MARCH

The army marched from the river Granicus south towards Sardis. The city was surrendered to him by Mithrenes, the Persian satrap. Alexander kept Mithrenes with him and gave him a position. He allowed the Lydian citizens to rule their city in the way they had ruled before the Persians came, but took the annual tribute, which had previously been paid to the Persians, for himself. He placed one of his Macedonians as satrap over the area. It was a pattern he repeated whenever he took a city.

Alexander's aim was to reach Halicarnassus before winter arrived. He sent small battle groups to pacify the hinterland and marched on to Ephesus, reaching it within three days.

He took the city, recalled those sent into exile for supporting him and forbade any citizens to carry out reprisals for past wrongs. His own political viewpoint was not something he foisted on the people he conquered. He had long since realized that leaving people with a choice bound them closer to him in loyalty. He exercised his power in Ephesus only to ensure that some of its citizens were not killed or driven out for the sake of revenge.

The army marched towards Miletus. News of its victory ran on ahead of them and most cities in its path opened their gates in surrender to Alexander or his commanders.

To encourage this, Alexander let it be known that his soldiers were banned from looting or raping and pillaging. He claimed that this was because he was already King of Asia and that he did not want his own property ruined.

The people of the cities and from the surrounding countryside expected to be enslaved by Alexander and were both astonished and delighted to discover that he pardoned them for fighting for the Persians. As he remarked: "They had no choice as they were enslaved by their Persian masters."

At the port of Miletus, the city refused to admit his army. They believed that the Persian navy would save them. Alexander, however, had already prepared for that. Before the Persian fleet of 400 triremes arrived, he had already contacted Nicanor, who brought the Greek navy of 160 triremes to anchor offshore, thus blocking the way into Miletus from the sea.

It was a time of omens and an eagle had been seen on a beach nearby. The soothsayers said it was a sign that victory would come by land. Or so Alexander told those of his commanders who were in favour of attacking the Persian navy.

Alexander appeared to be in luck again. A leading citizen offered to open the city to him. Alexander refused the offer and ordered the Greek fleet to continue to blockade the harbour to keep the Persian fleet from offering help. He then brought up the siege engines and started to besiege the city.

With the Greek navy threatening the city from the sea, Alexander had the town in a vice. Some of the Greek mercenaries defending the city were so desperate that, according to Arrian, "now despairing of safety, some of them cast themselves into the sea and lying upon their shields, escaped safe to a certain island whose name is unknown."

Alexander took the town and then turned his mind to dealing with the 300 Greek mercenaries who seemed to be willing to fight to the death on their island. He was much moved by their courage and offered not to move against them if they would agree to fight in his army. They agreed.

Perhaps this offer was designed to placate those Greeks on the mainland who felt he had been too harsh with the Greek mercenaries at Granicus.

By the time Miletus was taken, the Persian fleet had sailed away in search of fresh water.

Alexander's decision was vindicated. The essential weak point of the Persian naval power was its need to have ports in which to resupply its ships. All Alexander had to do to render them useless was to capture every base used by the Persians from the Hellespont to Halicarnassus and from Halicarnassus to Egypt.

Meanwhile in Halicarnassus (Bodrum), Memnon, who had been given command of lower Asia and the whole fleet by Darius, waited for Alexander – his nemesis.

On the march south, Alexander soon discovered that he was regarded as a benevolent victor. The Carians were a wild and formidable people with a reputation as fierce warriors. Alexander had no cause to fight them because they offered no opposition. He had been wise enough to bring Queen Ada, their traditional ruler, out of exile and to offer her back her throne. In gratitude, she asked if she could adopt him as her son and he agreed. He appointed her satrap of Caria and left 200 cavalry and a few thousand Greek mercenaries.

From then on the Carians gave him no trouble and he moved his army without opposition towards the port at Halicarnassus.

He ordered the Greek fleet to bring south, from Miletus, the battering rams, scaling ladders, catapults and the rest of the siege engines he believed he might need. Halicarnassus was powerfully defended by thick walls.

The siege was slow, but the Macedonian army gradually tightened the knot on the defenders. Alexander advanced towers from which archers shot into the city, he advanced sappers under cover to try to mine the walls, he attacked up siege ladders and with catapults firing huge

ABOVE *An armoured and moveable siege tower in action. Copper engraving, 1801.*

boulders. The wall was breached and then blocked by the defenders, who had built an inner curved wall to protect the city.

Alexander continued to rain down death from the catapults and high towers and even had a causeway built across the moat that protected the walls so that he could bring his siege towers closer to the city.

It was a fearful war of attrition and eventually it became clear to the defenders, Orontobates and Memnon, that the city could not sustain another assault. They decided to fire the city and then withdraw.

LEFT *Deep into the Turkish hinterland. The line of march towards the snow-covered Taurus Mountains.*

Alexander walked into the city, ordered his troops to kill anyone firing buildings, and not to molest the citizens. He left the Persian defenders in the citadel to which they had withdrawn and then razed the city to the ground.

The army should have rested in winter quarters. In five months, Alexander had beaten the Persian army in a set-piece battle, taken and secured the coastal cities and so begun to protect his supply line back to Macedonia. But still Alexander could not rest. He set out with a guerrilla band to close any options for the Persian fleet in the south of Asia Minor.

He felt secure enough by this time to order that all the newly married Macedonian soldiers should take home leave through the winter. He had, after all, recruited more men from the mercenary troops he had confronted on the march south. Soldiers know a lucky general when they see one and Alexander was not only lucky but skilful. His men loved him for his generosity in letting the young married men go home.

Parmenion took the siege engines and a party of returning Macedonian soldiers back to Sardis. He was to meet Alexander later in Gordium.

Alexander planned every move to ensure, as far as possible, the safety of his soldiers. He always secured his base before moving off on his next campaign. He knew that to secure his back he had to secure the hinterland and the high ground of the Anatolian plateau. As soon as the winter weather arrived, he marched the main part of his army north, towards the Black Sea, to subdue any opposition.

PLOTS AND WHISPERS

One afternoon Alexander was sleeping and woke annoyed at finding a swallow fluttering around his head and squawking loudly. It would dive away for a moment and then come back in a sweeping dive. It would hover, squawking even more loudly and dart off again. Alexander tried to sweep the bird away, but it came back again and again and finally landed on his head. It refused to go away until Alexander got up and walked out into the weak winter sunlight.

His seer told him that the bird was a warning. There was a problem coming from very close quarters. Someone who had reason to be grateful to him was plotting against him. But who and where was the plotter?

Parmenion supplied the answer. Alexander Lyncestes, brother of two men involved in the plot to kill Alexander's father, Philip, had been under suspicion at that time. Alexander refused to believe that his namesake, who was one of the first to proclaim support for Alexander's succession, could have been part of the plot to kill Philip. He even brought the young man into his companions, despite having his two brothers executed. Even at the time, Lyncestes was commanding the Thessalian cavalry.

Parmenion had captured a Persian envoy who had messages from Darius. He had confessed that he was taking a message to Alexander Lyncestes, offering him money and the kingdom of Macedonia if he would arrange for the murder of Alexander.

Parmenion had not yet revealed this situation to anyone else. Even Lyncestes was in complete ignorance that he was suspected of being involved in an assassination plot.

Alexander had to act quickly. He discussed the matter with his closest companions. They agreed it had been a mistake to put this man in charge of the Thessalian cavalry. He had to be removed with the least possible fuss. The Thessalian troops owed no blood allegiance to Alexander and there was a fear that they might be suborned by their general. It was imperative that no one should know about the threat until it had been neutralized.

Alexander called a close friend, Amophoterus, to his tent. He gave him a verbal message to take to Parmenion. To ensure complete secrecy, Amophoterus travelled in disguise with some native guides. He arrived at Parmenion's camp and delivered his message. Alexander Lyncestes was to be taken prisoner and isolated from his men immediately. He was to talk to no one.

It was done. For many months the prisoner was carried along by the army and only when the Thessalians had proved their worth, time and again, did Alexander have him executed.

WINTER 333BC.
THE MARCH INTO ANATOLIA AND THE GORDIAN KNOT

Alexander broke all the rules. By advancing in the teeth of winter snow and winds he pushed his army to their limit. It continued to be a campaign of lightning strikes and advances. He led his men into narrow mountain passes which were held by savage and determined tribesmen and defeated his enemies by a mixture of cunning and aggression.

If he was expected to emerge through a pass, he would order his engineers to make a path over mountains and emerge behind the enemy. He would appear to hesitate and throw the opposition troops off guard and then, with lightly armed, very fast-moving contingents of his army, he would attack with ruthless efficiency.

As far as possible he tried not to "live off the land", which ensured that even those he defeated respected him for leaving them enough food to survive in their harsh region.

Alexander knew that his army needed to regroup and rest. He had arranged to meet Parmenion further north towards Paphlagonia at the town of Gordium.

Parmenion arrived at the crossing of the river Sangarious where Gordium stood. He brought fresh troops with him. According to Arrian there were 3,000 Macedonian infantry men and 500 cavalry, including 300 Thessalians.

These new recruits joined the battle-hardened veterans in their camp near the river and below the walls of the city. Here was a place of omens, a place of legend, a place touched by myth.

According to the local people, Gordian held the answer to the mystery of who would rule Asia. Here was a prophesy that demanded a solution. Alexander was determined to provide it.

Gordium is said to have been the home of King Midas, who was reputed to turn anything he touched to gold. Alexander, however, was more interested in the prophesy that revolved around a simple chariot fastened to its yoke by a cord made from the bark of the cornel tree. The people of Gordium told him that according to prophecy the man who untied the knot would become the ruler of the whole world. Alexander went to see the chariot in the citadel and, driven by pride and his lust for power, said he would undo the knot.

There were friends and military leaders who were concerned at this. If Alexander now failed his men, who believed in the intervention of the gods in men's business, would feel afraid. They would believe that the gods were sending a message about his ambition and his chance of failure.

The fastenings were elaborately intertwined. They coiled one over the other and the ends were well hidden. For a time Alexander stared at the fastenings. Around him his generals began to look away in embarrassment and concern. He had to solve the problem. It was essential, yet he could not see where to begin. There are a number of stories about what happened next.

According to some, he found the ends of the cornel bark rope and simply undid it. According to Aristobulus, he merely removed the pin holding the yoke to the pole of the chariot and then pulled out the yoke. According to Plutarch, who wrote years after the event, he stared at it for a long time. He was aware of the concerns among his generals and the soldiers pressing to see what he would do.

He pulled at the rope for a time and nothing moved. He looked down across the plain to the river and saw the cooking fires of his men and knew he had no way out of the problem. He simply had to undo the knot.

LEFT *A romantic image of Alexander about to solve the problem of the Gordian knot.*

He saw from the concern in the faces of his soldiers that this was a turning point. He had to undo this knot to have a chance of fulfilling the prophecy.

He stood back from the knot and heard the sharp intake of breath from his dear friend Hephaestion who stood at his shoulder. Alexander lost his temper, drew his short sword and slashed once across the knot. It fell apart. Alexander had undone the knot.

Arrian reported that he was unsure how Alexander had solved the problem of the Gordian

ABOVE *Ruins looking across to the Taurus Mountains.*

knot, but whatever he had done, the gods seemed to approve. Zeus thundered across the sky that night and white flickers of lightning lit the whole horizon and the mountains beyond the river.

The army rested in camp until May, when the season for war began again.

Alexander knew that his greatest rival, Memnon, was leading the Persian navy in its campaign to try to block Alexander's support from Athens and the Greek city-states. He had to address the problem of the Persian navy's supply lines once and for all.

He turned south from Gordium, across the river Halys and, skirting the mountains and the highland of Cappadocia, pushed across the Phrygian plain towards the Taurus Mountains, through the pass known as the Cilicean Gates. Unknowingly, Alexander was nearing his first confrontation with Darius, the Persian king.

The summer in the south of Turkey is fierce. Alexander's army has been calculated to have needed 100,000 gallons (455,000 litres) of water a day and most of the rivers in the area would have been reduced to a trickle by the oppressive heat. Alexander forced the pace of the army and they had to subsist on tight rations.

As they marched through the arid land, the peoples who lived there submitted to the invaders, getting the best terms they could. These terms often included the supply of provisions to be dumped for the army on their line of march.

It was spring in 333BC and Memnon, who had little success in changing the loyalty of Athens, died at sea. Alexander heard of his death and felt this gave him time to turn and invade Cilicia before addressing the problem of the Persian army, which intelligence reports now led him to believe was approaching the Syrian coast.

Tactically, Alexander knew he needed to cover his rear by subduing Cilicia, before taking on the Persian army.

He took an advance guard of lightly armed infantry men and archers and led them to the Cilicean Gates. The narrow pass was heavily guarded by Persian soldiers, but when they saw the approaching flying column of soldiers they turned and fled.

Alexander took Tarsus and stopped its Persian satrap from looting it. Here it is believed that he contracted malaria which laid him low for nearly two months.

It had taken the army just over 30 days to march from Gordium to Tarsus through the terrible heat of summer.

Alexander was feverish, shaking with ague and sometimes rambling in his mind. His doctors were terrified to treat him. Some said he was too ill to treat, others were afraid that if they treated him and he died that then they would be blamed.

Alexander had an old friend called Philip, from Acarnia. He had medical skills and believed it was his duty to try to save Alexander from death. He prepared a draught for Alexander.

As Alexander lay in his tent sweating and sometimes delirious he received a letter from Parmenion warning him to beware of Philip. Parmenion had learned that Darius had promised Philip large amounts of money and marriage to his daughter if he would kill Alexander.

Philip crossed the open ground carrying a phial of liquid. He passed the guards and went

DARIUS' DREAM

Plutarch records a dream that Darius had while marching towards the coast of Cilicia from Susa.

Darius was confident that his army of 600,000 men had the beating of the upstart Alexander. His Magi (wise men) had interpreted a dream he had in such a way that he was pleased. Darius believed the Magi had told him he would defeat the invaders.

He had dreamed that he saw the Macedonian phalanx encircled with flames and Alexander waiting on him dressed as a servant in a cloak he had once worn when he was a royal messenger. Then Alexander had entered the temple of Belos and disappeared.

Plutarch suggested that what the dream really meant was that Alexander would rule and Darius would soon lose his glory and die. Hindsight, however, is a wonderful help in prophecy.

into the dimly lit tent. Alexander was lying on a litter, propped up by pillows. His forehead shimmered with sweat. He looked across at Philip who told him he had brought him some medicine to break the fever.

Alexander took the phial and as he did so he handed Parmenion's warning letter to Philip. Philip took the letter and began to read. He was horrified. He knew that these accusations meant he would die. He looked across at Alexander and watched in astonishment as his old friend drank the liquid in the phial. Alexander looked across at Philip and smiled.

"Trust your friends with your life."

Very soon Alexander had the litter carried outside the tent and his soldiers came to rejoice at the sight of their general alive and well. The time for battle had come again.

LEFT *Asclepius treating a patient. A stone relief. Fifth-century BC.*

CHAPTER SIX

A BATTLE, A SIEGE
AND AN OMEN

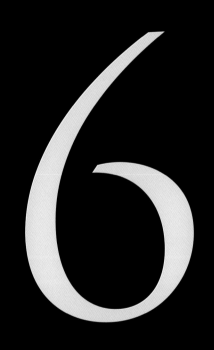

6

AFTER THE BATTLE OF GRANICUS KING DARIUS OF PERSIA MOVED TOWARDS THE COAST TO LINK UP WITH HIS NAVY. ALEXANDER ANTICIPATED DARIUS' NEXT MOVE AND SENT THE THESSALIAN CAVALRY AND GREEK AND BALKAN INFANTRYMEN TO REMOVE ALL PERSIAN TROOPS FROM THE COASTAL STRIP AS FAR SOUTH AS THE PASS OF JONAH.

AFTER DISPATCHING PARMENION AND THE
THESSALIAN CAVALRY AND GREEK AND BALKAN INFANTRYMEN
TO THE SOUTH COAST, ALEXANDER THEN TOOK THE REST OF HIS
FORCE WEST. HERE HE SUBDUED ANY CITIES WHO FAVOURED THE
PERSIAN RULER. IN SET-PIECE BATTLES AND BY USING FLYING COLUMNS,
HE BLOCKED DARIUS' ROUTE TO HIS NAVAL FORCES. ALEXANDER LEFT
HIS SICK AND WOUNDED TO RECOVER BY THE RIVER ISSUS AND, AFTER
THANKING THE GODS WITH SACRIFICES AND GAMES IN THEIR
HONOUR, HE MOVED TO JOIN PARMENION.

BUT WHERE WAS THE MAIN PERSIAN ARMY? WHERE WAS DARIUS THE
GREAT KING? COULD ALEXANDER HAVE MISSED THEM ON THE MARCH?

A BATTLE NEEDS TWO OPPOSING FORCES AND ALEXANDER AND
DARIUS SEEMED TO HAVE MISPLACED EACH OTHER. THE WEATHER WAS
HARSH AND WIND AND RAIN SLOWED UP ALEXANDER'S MOVEMENTS. HE
RESTED HIS MEN FOR A DAY AND A NIGHT.

IT SEEMS THE TWO ARMIES HAD MARCHED ON OPPOSITE SIDES OF A
RANGE OF MOUNTAINS AND IN OPPOSITE DIRECTIONS.

Alexander offered sacrifice in thanks to Athene and then heard that Darius and his huge army were at Sochi – two days' march away. This turned out to be untrue. What was true was that Darius was so confident about defeating Alexander that he had brought along his family with the royal party.

Alexander moved to engage Darius in the firm belief that his army was only a short distance away. In fact, Darius had moved into Alexander's last camp and slaughtered the wounded and incapacitated Macedonians that Alexander had left behind as unfit for service. Before he had them killed, Darius had the wounded mutilated.

Plutarch reports that Alexander was shocked to find the Persian king and his army at his rear. He did not believe it could be true. He ordered some of his companions – his most favoured friends – to go on a spying mission. They were under strict orders that under no circumstances should they allow themselves to be seen by the enemy.

Arrian reports that Alexander ordered a picked group to "... take a galley along the coast towards the Issus. Find out if it [the presence of the Persian army] can be true. And discover the disposition of the Persian army."

The galley slipped in and out of the indented coastline, careful not to be seen. It was true. The Persians were at Issus. The galley raced back to give Alexander the news.

It was now that Alexander showed his genius as a commander of men. He knew that their line of retreat was cut off by Darius. It was now a matter of life or death. It had been raining for some time, his men were cold and wet and their spirits were low.

He called together his cavalry and his infantry officers, the leaders of the Cretan bowmen, his companion bodyguard and the officers in charge of the Thracians, Paeonians, Illyrians and Agrianes – his foreign troops.

He looked around the battle-hardened faces before him. Many of the officers had fought for his father and had known him as a boy. They knew the danger they were in as well as he did. It continued to rain. They sat and he began to speak quietly to them.

He told them that they were all a very long way from home, and that there had been many battles, one battle after another, on the journey to Issus. But Darius had to be defeated if Alexander was to go on. It was November 333BC and Alexander was just 23 years old.

Alexander had taken his share of the hardships and the older men, who sat watching, knew him for what he was. Alexander waited a moment and then spoke again.

"Remember that you have already faced danger and looked it triumphantly in the face. You have won great victories and the enemy has already been beaten once. It seems the gods are on our side, for Darius is in the wrong position to make a fight of it."

From the scouts he had sent out he knew the dispositions of the Persian army. Darius' left wing was hemmed in by the steep sides of the river valley and his right was constricted by the line of the coast.

For some reason Darius had chosen to fight a defensive battle. Alexander found this inexplicable, considering the vast superiority of the Persian forces. Once more his luck held.

Darius would be unable to deploy his cavalry with any effect and, because he had so many infantry, they were too tightly bunched and on too short a line.

Alexander went on. "We will break through and chaos will be the result. Darius wants to fight a defensive battle and to let us break against his fortifications. We will not oblige him."

The veterans in front of him laughed. Someone asked about the Greek mercenaries who were fighting for Darius and Alexander was scornful.

"They have no cause worth fighting for. They fight for money and not much of that. We fight for Greece and our hearts will be in it. As for you men of Thrace or Illyria, all our foreign allies are the best and finest soldiers in Europe." Alexander looked over them and smiled. His commanders stood and raised their arms in salute as they acclaimed their commander.

"Remember," he said quietly. "The great King Darius is commanding his army in person. Once he has been swept away nothing can stop us from taking the whole of his kingdom and all of its wealth."

He dismissed the commanders and ordered that the men were to be well fed before preparing themselves to move to confront Darius' army 12 miles (19 kilometres) or so away. The rain continued to fall on his exhausted men.

Alexander sent out scouts to check the pass down through the mountains to the river below. It was unguarded. Darius clearly believed Alexander would not move for a time.

Alexander took the army through the pass by midnight and waited there. Then, Arrian writes: "As soon as dawn appeared he began to descend from the hills, having straitened his front by reason of the narrowness of the pass."

As the mountains began to open Alexander dispatched his army one part after another, into a close and regular phalanx … the right wing extending to the mountains and the left to the sea shore."

He had already discussed and agreed the order of battle. On the right wing, three battalions of guards under Nicanor were on slightly rising ground, Coenus' battalion, on their left, was in close touch with Perdicca's men. In the centre, he placed the heavy infantry. On the left were Amyanta's troops, then Ptolemy's and then Meleager's battalion. Command of the infantry on the left was given to Craterus and the whole of the left wing went to Parmenion.

Alexander reminded them that they must not allow a gap between the extreme left and the sea or there would be a risk that Darius' cavalry might outflank them.

As usual, Alexander gave his commanders an overall view of how the battle was to be conducted, but gave each of them the latitude to react to events as they happened. In this way, in the mayhem of the fighting, the army became a flexible weapon that responded swiftly without the need to wait for orders from the supreme commander.

By this time the enemy position would have been in view. Darius made some changes to his position, shifted men to cover the flanks and moved all his cavalry to the right wing, near the shore.

His plan seems to have been to engage Alexander's phalanx on the left with his cavalry. To break it and rout it. Alexander moved his army steadily towards the river and the front line of the Persian army. He redeployed his cavalry to reply to the threat of the Persian cavalry, moved his archers and protected his right with the Agrianian horsemen. All this as he continued to move steadily, remorselessly, into the face of the enemy.

From time to time Alexander ordered a halt. Under no circumstances would he allow the line to become confused.

The enemy positions on the river bank were protected in some places by hurriedly built stockades and in others by the steep banks ... The Greeks came steadily on. The two armies could now see each other's faces.

They knew that when the struggle came, the fighting would be hand to hand and desperate.

Alexander would have to take his army across the river in full view and range of the front ranks of Darius and his infantry and archers. He halted his men once more and spoke to them all.

ABOVE *A Persian archer ready and waiting to attack the Macedonians. From a relief at Tackt-i-Bostan in Iran.*

"Our enemies are Medes and Persians.
They are men who have lived soft lives. We are men trained in the violent school of war. We are all freemen and those men over there are slaves. You see the Greeks who fight for Darius over there. They only fight for money. We have a greater cause. Freedom. And who leads you ... Alexander! And who leads those soft men ... Darius!"

And his men cheered his words. He knew how to touch their hearts and to take away the fear all men feel before charging into a hail of javelins and arrows. The men laughed and cheered him.

Plutarch tells us: "He rode with words of encouragement for all, addressing by name, remembering individuals' ranks and distinctions, not the officers of highest rank only, but the captains of squadrons and companies; even the mercenaries were not forgotten where any distinction or act called for the mention of a name. From every throat came the answering shout ... 'Wait no longer. Forward!'"

Alexander answered them by turning and lifting his arm. Mounted on his horse, Bucephalus, his sparkling burnished silver helmet catching the light, he moved his arm forward and down.

The Macedonian army's assault on the Persians began almost imperceptibly. They edged forward slowly, keeping their dressing, allowing no gaps to develop, they moved towards the river which sparkled in the sunlight. Metal clanked on metal, swords unsheathed, bowmen knocking their first arrows to the bowstring, they marched steadily forward. Eyes straining forward, no man swerving and holding back, ready to take on the spears and arrows of the enemy.

Alexander held the line steady. The commanders knew their work. They were accustomed to battle and knew their men were ready for whatever the Fates threw at them. This was the fighting machine Alexander led into the face of the Persian army.

Slowly Alexander picked up speed. As he led the right wing it became a gallop. Into the stream, across it and into the roaring maelstrom of battle.

The assault now relied on speed more than power. The Persian archers ran, but before they could be protected by the men behind them, Alexander and his cavalry were on them and were merciless. The impetuous charge was nearly the undoing of Alexander. He had drawn in the two battalions of the phalanx on the right with him. They picked up speed and this meant that the four left battalions under Parmenion, still advancing steadily, holding their line.

Arian described it: "The Persians attempting to push the Macedonians back into the river were trying to snatch victory from their hands. The Macedonians, on the other hand, striving to snatch the conquest they had so nearly achieved. They fought for the glory of the phalanx which had never been broken and refused to allow the phalanx to be dishonoured by defeat."

The Persian's Greek mercenaries moved fast into the breaking phalanx and threw them back into the river. Alexander saw the situation and immediately wheeled his cavalry and the rest of the phalanx and attacked the Greek mercenaries on their flank.

On the left of the Macedonian front, Parmenion was having a hard struggle against the Persian cavalry, but in the confusion of battle it was learned that Darius and his bodyguard had

LEFT *The archers of the royal guard of Darius the First. Relief sculpture in Persepolis.*

ALEXANDER M. DARIVM VLT: SVPERAT
CA SIS IN ACIE PERSAR: PEDIT: CM. EQVIT
VI. RO. X. M. INTERFECTIS. MATRE QVOQVE
CONIVGE. LIBERIS DARII REG: CVM M. HAVD
AMPLIVS EQVITIB: FVGA DILAPSI. CAPTIS.

already taken their chariots out of the line and had run from the thrusting spears and swords that continued to advance on them without their leader. The Persian army broke in blind panic.

The coming of night was the only thing that saved the Persian forces from being totally wiped out. Alexander's men harried and chased and cut down as many men as they could. Alexander wanted Darius taken alive, but he was nowhere to be found. He had to be satisfied with capturing Darius' beautiful wife, daughters, his mother and mother-in-law.

In fleeing the battle of Issus, Darius had abandoned not only his army, but also his family. Plutarch describes the scene when Alexander went into the enemy camp. "His army was carrying off loot from the Persians. The Persian army had left most of its baggage in Damascus so that they could travel light, but Darius' quarters were full of treasures, luxurious furniture and lavishly dressed servants. These had all been set aside by the advancing cavalry for Alexander."

As soon as he arrived, still covered in the sweat and filth of battle and nursing a dagger thrust in his thigh, he stripped off his armour and said: "Let's wash off the sweat of battle in Darius' bath."

"No, my lord," said one of the companions. "In Alexander's bath now."

In the bathroom Alexander saw the most beautifully crafted basins and pitchers, the baths themselves and caskets full of perfumes all made of intricately worked Sythian gold. He walked into the dining area and found magnificent couches and tables.

"So!" he said, "This, it seems, is what it is to be a king."

It was as he began to eat that Alexander learned that Darius' family had been taken prisoner. He was told that when they saw the bow that Darius had left in his chariot in his flight they had cried out, supposing him dead.

For a time Alexander was quiet, moved by the grief they must have been feeling. Then he sent Leonatus, a childhood friend, to tell them that Darius was not dead and that they need have no fear. He assured them they would be treated as was fitting for the family of a king. He also gave them permission to bury as many Persians as they wished and to keep those clothes and ornaments they wanted.

ABOVE *While the Battle of Issus rages around him, King Darius and his bodyguard take to their chariots and retreat, leaving the Persian army in a frenzy.*

LEFT *The Battle of Issus, painted by Altdorfer Albrecht in 1529, depicting the victory of Alexander the Great over the Persians under Darius III.*

ALEXANDER'S DISCIPLINE

"But the most honorable and truly regal service which he [Alexander] rendered to these chaste and noble women was to ensure that they should never hear, suspect nor have cause to fear anything which could disgrace them … They were guarded as if they were virgin priestesses, rather than women in an enemy camp."

Alexander's response to the women from Darius' family was remarkable considering the usual fate of women prisoners. More remarkable yet considering that the queen, Darius' wife, was said to be the most beautiful woman in Asia and that her daughters were very like her. The fact that Darius had abandoned them on the battlefield says much about him. He would have known that such beautiful women would become prized possessions of the conquering king.

There was one woman, in particular, who did attract Alexander. Barsine, the widow of Memnon – taken prisoner by Parmenion in Damascus. She was gentle, Greek-educated and of Persian royal descent. Legend says that Alexander's first son, Heracles, was born to her.

Alexander treated Darius' family with great honour. When he met them first he said to his great friend Hephaestion: "These Persian women are a torment for our eyes," and was determined to practice self-control when they were near him. Indeed, it is said that he avoided them as much as possible.

There were those who knew he enjoyed young and good-looking men about him and many young slave boys were offered to him as gifts. He was offered some by a merchant from Tarentum. He was furious and asked his friends if they had detected signs of degeneracy in him that he should be offered slaves of this sort.

Two soldiers serving with Parmenion were discovered to have seduced the wives of Greek mercenaries. Alexander ordered that if the men were found guilty they should be put to death as wild beasts who preyed on mankind. He could be very harsh.

He once told Queen Ada, who had adopted him, that the sweetmeats she sent him were unnecessary. He had been taught by Leonidas, his first tutor, that the best cook was a night march.

"Leonidas used to examine the chests and wardrobes in which my bedding and clothes were put in case some forbidden luxury should be smuggled there by my mother."

Plutarch claims that he used to say that "sex and sleep were things that made him most sensible of his mortality". So he controlled his desires.

Parmenion was sent to Damascus to guard the property which had been left behind by Darius when he fled. Parmenion led the Thessalian cavalry, whom Alexander had singled out after their brave display in the battle. They should have the first pickings of the loot in the city. Parmenion was astonished at the luxury he found there. There was so much, according to Plutarch, that "there was enough to make the whole army rich. The Macedonians having once tasted the treasures and luxuries of the barbarians hunted for the Persian wealth with all the ardour of hounds upon the scent."

Parmenion sent a list of the items to Alexander: "Apart from vast quantities of gold ornaments and coins there are 329 female musicians and singers, 46 garland weavers, 277 kitchen workers, 29 chefs, 40 perfume makers, 70 wine warmers as well as purple cloth, ivory and other treasures."

There were also ambassadors from various Greek cities. Athens, Thebes and Sparta had representatives at the abandoned court. Alexander ordered that the Thebans be released, for they had good reason to plot against him.

The Athenians were to be sent home, as if they were of no importance to Alexander. He arrested the Spartans, who were representatives of the most dangerous city on the Greek mainland, and then, recognizing their political status, he sent them freely home.

Alexander was a leader in complete military and diplomatic control. He regrouped his army and marched south. Alexander had business in Egypt, but before he arrived there he had other obstacles to overcome.

THE SIEGE OF TYRE (332BC)

Leaving Darius and the battered remnants of his army to flee into Persia, Alexander turned back towards the Mediterranean coast. Persian power still held, down through Syria, through the Phoenician city of Tyre, down to Gaza and into Egypt. Tyre and Gaza were both used to resupply the Persian navy and Alexander knew that to defeat the Persians this had to change.

He resolved to sweep down into Egypt and then, having wiped out all threats to his rear, he could turn back and advance into Asia with some security.

It is a mark of the man that he refused to take the simple option and to chase after Darius into the hinterland. No doubt he could have routed the Persian army again and maybe even captured Darius, but he preferred to advance only when his bases were secure. It was in this way that he could feel secure without his army feeling that its line of retreat was fatally overstretched.

As he advanced on Tyre he took other cities, thereby removing the threat of attack. He met a delegation from Tyre who were willing to let him pass by without any trouble.

ALEXANDER EXPLAINS HIS REASONS

"Friends and fellow soldiers, I do not see how we can safely advance upon Egypt, so long as Persia controls the sea; and to pursue Darius with the neutral city of Tyre in our rear and Egypt and Cyprus still in enemy hands would be a serious risk, especially in view of the serious situation in Greece."

Alexander knew very well that the city-states would not take much provocation to turn on him in Macedonia.

"With our army on the track of Darius far inland in the direction of Babylon, the Persians might well regain control of the coast, and thus be enabled, with more power behind them, to transfer the war to Greece, where Sparta is already openly hostile to us and Athens, at the moment, is an unwilling ally; fear, not friendliness, keeps her on our side. With Tyre destroyed, all Phoenicia would be ours, and the Phoenician fleet, which both in numbers and quality is the predominant element in the sea power of Persia, would very likely come over to us. Once their towns are in our hands, the Phoenician seamen, ships, crews or fighting men, will hardly wish to face the perils of service at sea for the sake of others. The next step will be Cyprus. It will either join us without trouble or be easily taken by assault. Then our supremacy at sea would be guaranteed. With Egypt in our hands we have no need for uneasiness about Greece. We shall be able to march on Babylon with security at home, with enhanced prestige and with Persia excluded, not only from the sea, but from the whole continent as far east as the Euphrates."

Alexander wanted more than that. He wanted to worship in the temple in the city. This the delegation had to refuse, because no outsiders were allowed to worship there.

It may have been the excuse he needed. Whatever the reason, he called up all his siege engines and began a systematic assault on Tyre. Seven months later it would surrender.

The siege of Tyre was not easy. The city was built on an island, strongly defended by huge ramparts and by the Persian navy. Alexander's plan was to use his engineers to build a causeway across the shallow water between the shore and the town. His engineers would do this by using local materials. The work began.

Alexander was, according to Arrian, "… always present … He designed everything himself and saw everything done. He encouraged those who seemed to slacken and commended others who progressed their work eagerly."

The Tyrians mocked the idea at first and continually harassed the working parties both from the sea and from the ramparts. But Alexander ordered up two towers – in the top of each he placed artillery, catapults and also archers to bombard the city.

The Tyrians sent a fire ship loaded with pitch and sulphur and had her towed to the towers on the causeway and burned the siege towers where they stood. They pitched huge boulders into the sea around the walls to keep away the siege ships that carried scaling ladders and assault towers to attack the walls.

Alexander gave orders to enlarge the causeway and to rebuild the siege towers while he and his guards brought his own warships from Sidon into the battle. As the ships were being made ready, Alexander went into Arabia and subdued an area there, to cover his flank.

He returned to Sidon, took on a contingent of Greek mercenaries and sailed to attack the Persian fleet off Tyre. He also had with him the Phoenician commanders and the Cypriot navy, who had gone over to him, just as he had predicted.

The enemy fleet refused to engage in battle and blocked the harbour at Tyre.

Alexander ordered the total blockade of the city from both land and sea and also continued regular assaults on the 150-foot-high (46-metre) city walls. As that struggle went on, Alexander decided to try to remove the blockage caused by the huge stones that had been thrown into the channel by which his ships would have to advance on the city.

His men tried to get block and tackle onto the submerged boulders while the Tyrians sent specially armed boats to attack Alexander's triremes by cutting their anchor ropes. Then they sent in divers, who cut the ships free from their anchors, thus causing chaos on the decks.

The triremes then had to use chain instead of rope. It was a game of cat and mouse, but slowly Alexander's ships closed on the city walls.

The Tyrians then manned 13 ships with their most experienced men and moved out silently at night until they came onto the Cypriot ships and assaulted them. Alexander ordered the entire fleet into battle as the Tyrian ships broke clear. They forced the Tyrian ships back. Now Alexander increased the pressure on the landward side. He also ordered the ships close under the city walls to use their artillery to damage the walls and to engage the attention of the defenders inside. It was a desperate struggle. Alexander wanted to go on down into Egypt, but Tyre was determined not to be taken easily.

At last a breach was made in the walls. Alexander then manned ships with fighting men and placed aboard the wooden gangways they had made. As they came close to the city walls where the defences were weakest, the gangways were lowered and his men poured into the breach. Led by Admetus, in command of the first wave of attackers, they stormed over the walls. Admetus was killed by a spear on this first assault, but Alexander took control and soon sections of the wall were under his command.

What happened then is a measure of the anger Alexander felt at the delay he had suffered at the hands of the Tyrian defenders and the insult he felt they had offered him by refusing to let him worship in their temple. The anger of his men was whipped up according to Arrian because "the Tyrians had taken some prisoners, hauled them up aloft upon their walls in sight of their friends, afterwards stabbed them and threw their bodies into the sea."

The soldiers who saw this were driven into a killing frenzy because their comrades had been denied an honourable death or, much worse, an honourable burial.

Alexander had 2,000 able-bodied men crucified on the approaches to the city, his soldiers went on a killing rampage and only those who had taken refuge in the temple were spared death. Thirty thousand men, women and children were sold into slavery.

It was midsummer when Tyre fell and at about this time Darius made his first attempt to negotiate peace. He offered one of his daughters in marriage, vast amounts of gold and all the land west of the Euphrates. Parmenion said that if he was Alexander he would accept it. Alexander replied that if he were Parmenion so would he.

This response to the advice of his oldest and most experienced general shows the beginnings of strains between the old soldiers who had fought for Philip and the younger blood Alexander had promoted. It was an inevitable and difficult problem. Alexander knew that he had to hold the very different interests together. However, he was not going to accept any offer from Darius.

Alexander, in reply, told him that he would marry Darius' daughter when and if he liked and without asking Darius for permission. He also he told Darius that when he wrote again he should address him as Ruler of Persia, for Darius was no longer its king.

Apart from a month-long siege of Gaza, the way was now open for Alexander's army to sweep into Egypt which waited for a king who would rid them of their Persian overlords.

In November 332BC, Alexander was welcomed by the Egyptians as their saviour. He worshipped at the temple of Ptah in Memphis and, unlike the Persians, who had pillaged the Egyptian places of worship, he honoured their gods.

While any foreign army was an army of occupation, Alexander did his best to ensure that Egypt did not feel the hatred it had felt for the oppressive rule exerted by the Persians.

ABOVE *The Greek navy denied the Persians freedom at sea as they closed in on Tyre's city walls.*

ALEXANDER'S CASKET

One of the most beautiful pieces taken from the hoard left behind by Darius in Damascus was a casket. It may have been of Sythian workmanship – gold and ivory and with exquisite inlays. It was sent to Alexander and he asked his friends what they thought was worthy to go into such a box. Plutarch wrote: "Different things were proposed but Alexander said that he would put into it his most valued possession. He took his copy of Homer's *Iliad* and put it into the box."

And as the hero of the *Iliad* is Achilles, ancestor of Alexander, maybe that should not come as such a surprise.

The priests regarded him as Pharaoh and there were some who worshipped him. Here was the first hint that he might decide that he should be regarded as a god. It was not something that would endear him to the Macedonians in his army nor, particularly, to the older officers. The younger commanders flattered him by accepting the situation, which encouraged him to feel he was more than a mere mortal.

Alexander decided to visit the shrine of Ammon at the oasis in Siwah. The oracle there had the reputation of always being right. Alexander also wanted to go there because it was said that Perseus and Heracles had consulted it. Alexander believed that their blood flowed in his veins and also that, in some way, through his descent from Zeus, he was also descended from Ammon.

Arrian tells us that he was determined to get more precise information on the subject ... or at least to say that he had obtained it. A slightly cynical view of his subject perhaps.

He marched 200 miles (322 kilometres) along the coast and the desert route was hazardous. There was little water to be had and high winds sometimes totally obliterated the track. Plutarch tells us that once an army went on the same journey and when the wind come up 50,000 men were lost under the swirling sand.

Indeed, it is claimed that Alexander and his men lost their way, could not see the stars, could find no track or landmark ... nothing to identify where they were. But the gods rescued him, Ptolemy wrote, when two snakes led the army, hissing as they went. They led the way to the oracle and back to Memphis across the desert again.

Aristobulous says there were two crows who showed the way. Arrian is sure that somehow the gods intervened and saved him and remarks that "precisely what form it took we shall never know because of the disparity in the various records". Maybe Arrian was right.

SIWAH AND THE ORACLE

The shrine at Siwah could be found in a small oasis five miles (eight kilometres) wide at its broadest point. Fruit trees and olives grew there. It is an unusual fact that the water in the spring grew cooler through the morning and as evening came became warmer again.

It seems that the gods were with Alexander, for he came to the shrine and was welcomed on Ammon's behalf by the priests, as a god greeting his son!

Alexander asked the oracle if all of Philip's murderers had been accounted for and was assured that they had been. He then asked if he would rule over the world and was assured that he would. Alexander gave huge sums of money to the priests and adopted the worship of Ammon, his father.

Alexander had the answers he wanted, or at least he said he had, and there was no one who could deny it.

On his return from Siwah to Memphis some writers noted that Alexander began to behave haughtily, as if convinced of his divinity. To the Greeks and his army he was careful not to pretend to be a god.

Plutarch wrote, "Alexander did not allow himself to become vain or foolishly conceited because of his belief in his divinity, but rather used it to assert his authority over others." His behaviour did, however, sow the first seeds of unrest that would lead to plots against him in the future. He rejoined the main body of his army at Memphis

In the spring the Macedonian army marched north. Alexander was determined to destroy Darius once and for all. The time was right, his lines of supply were secure, his army was well rested, the Gods were happy and Alexander was impatient to become ruler of the world. Not for his own good, he would claim, but for the good of all men … all nations. He was not yet 25 years old.

ALEXANDRIA — DREAM OF A CITY

It was April 331BC when Alexander founded the city still named after him.

It is said that he wanted the city he built to be a port and one night he dreamed that he saw a grey-haired man standing reciting these lines from the *Odyssey*: "Out of the tossing sea where it breaks on the Egyptian beaches, Rises an island from the water and the name men give it is Pharos."

Alexander woke the next morning went to the lighthouse known as Pharos and saw the perfect site for his city. "Mark it out," he ordered the architects he had brought with him from Macedonia. They had no powdered chalk to mark the ground and so they took barley meal, marked out a semi-circle on the dark earth and also marked the outlines of the city and the plan of the streets in grids. The street plan of Alexandria is much the same today.

As they spread the barley, huge flocks of ibis, flamingoes and other migrating birds clattered into the air off the lagoon and settled and ate up the barley meal.

Alexander was very worried and asked diviners that he trusted to explain what it meant. They reassured him that the birds were an omen that the city would not only have riches enough, but that the citizens would come from many nations. Who is to say they were wrong?

BELOW *An artist's impression of ancient Alexandria, the first city of that name founded by Alexander the Great.*

CHAPTER SEVEN

BABYLON, SUSA AND PERSEPOLIS

FOLLOWING THE SIEGE OF TYRE, ALEXANDER CONTROLLED THE MEDITERRANEAN SEA BY DENYING THE PERSIAN FLEET ACCESS TO PORTS ALONG THE MIDDLE-EASTERN SEABOARD AND INTO ANATOLIA. HE RULED AS FAR SOUTH AS EGYPT, BUT HE STILL HAD NOT CONQUERED PERSIA.

YET, WHEN ALEXANDER WROTE TO REJECT DARIUS' OFFER OF PEACE, THE HAND OF HIS DAUGHTER AND THE VAST AMOUNTS OF GOLD, HE WROTE AS IF HE CONTROLLED THE WHOLE OF ASIA:

"KING ALEXANDER TO DARIUS, THAT DARIUS, WHOSE NAME YOU HAVE TAKEN, DEVASTATED THE GREEK COLONIES IN IONIA AND THE COAST OF THE HELLESPONT ALSO INHABITED BY GREEKS AND THEN INVADED THE MAINLAND OF MACEDONIA AND GREECE. THEN CAME XERXES OF THE SAME FAMILY WHO ATTACKED US AGAIN, PILLAGED OUR CITIES AND BURNT OUR FIELDS. WHO DOES NOT KNOW THAT MY FATHER WAS ASSASSINATED BY THOSE YOU CORRUPTED WITH YOUR MONEY? ... THE GODS, ALWAYS FAIR TO THE JUST, HAVE ALREADY GIVEN ME A VICTORY OVER YOU. YOU HAVE NO CLAIM ON MY KINDNESS, BUT IF YOU COME AS A SUPPLICANT I PROMISE YOU SHALL GET YOUR WIFE AND CHILDREN AND YOUR MOTHER WITHOUT RANSOM. DO YOU FEAR TO PUT YOURSELF IN OUR POWER? IF SO, YOU MAY HAVE HOSTAGES FROM US TO SECURE YOUR SAFETY. IN FUTURE, WHEN YOU WRITE TO ME, REMEMBER THAT YOU ARE NOT ADDRESSING MERELY A KING, BUT YOUR KING."

(QUINTUS CURTIUS, THE HISTORY OF ALEXANDER THE GREAT, TRANSLATED BY PETER PRATT, 1821)

Strong words considering that Alexander had yet to make a move into the Persian Empire beyond the Euphrates.

The terms of the offer had been discussed by Alexander and his senior officers and there was unease amongst these more experienced men at the cavalier way in which Alexander rejected it.

He claimed that he wanted to defeat the Persian powers which had threatened the Hellenic civilization since the days of Xerxes. He knew he had to move his army into unknown territory.

Syria, Egypt, Mesopotamia and the Turkish coast were areas that the Greeks knew and had settled in from time to time. Alexander had retaken this territory, but now he faced the daunting prospect of marching against a Persian army which Darius had already regrouped and reinforced with cavalry from the tribes in the Persian hinterland. Alexander advanced into the wide-open plains where the next "killing fields" would be. He was determined to engage and defeat the Persians under Darius once and for all.

As Alexander's army of 40,000 infantrymen and several thousand cavalry marched through the summer heat, Darius' captive wife, Statira, died in childbirth. One of her servants, a eunuch called Teircos, escaped, stole a horse and raced across country to the Persian lines and asked for an audience with King Darius.

Plutarch wrote: "When Darius heard of her death, he beat his head and broke into floods of tears. After which he cried out: 'Ah the cruel fate of the Persians. Was the wife and sister of their king not only taken captive, but after her death to be deprived of the ceremonies and mourning due to her high rank.'"

The eunuch answered: "As to the mourning and burial, my lord, all the honours the queen had a right to claim were given to her. For neither my mistress Statira, during her life, nor your royal mother or the children, missed any advantages of their former fortune except that of seeing the light of your face. Far from being deprived of any of the solemnities of her funeral, the queen was honoured with the tears of her very enemies. Alexander is as mild in the use of his victories as he is terrible in battle."

Darius was very deeply moved by these words and took the eunuch into his private rooms to question him more closely. He asked: "Tell me, as you honour me your king, is it not true that the death of Statira is the least of her misfortunes I have to lament. Did she not suffer terrible things while she lived?

ABOVE *A marble head of Alexander the Great.*

RIGHT *A stone relief showing two rulers of Persia, Darius I (left) and his successor Xerxes I (right).*

ABOVE *The river Tigris which Alexander and his army marched towards as they made their way to Guagamela.*

What, apart from her disgrace, could make a young man treat with such honour the wife of his enemy?"

The eunuch knelt and begged his king not to "… use expressions so unworthy of himself, so injurious to Alexander and so dishonourable to the memory of his wife and sister." He then explained that "Alexander is more admired for his decency to the Persian women than for his courage in battle."

Darius was most impressed and grateful. He even suggested, according to Plutarch, that if he did not defeat Alexander then he hoped that Alexander would be the next to sit on the Persian throne.

Alexander marched on with his army and hoped to cross the Euphrates at Thapsacus, near the coast. There, 3,000 men, under the command of Mazaeus, had been ordered by Darius to prevent his advance, or at least to slow him down.

Alexander had sent engineers ahead and they had half-constructed two bridges. They did not finish them in case the Persians used them to cross and attack their bridgehead and the advancing army.

As soon as news came to the engineers that Alexander was approaching with his army they completed the bridges and the Persians fled.

The army then turned northeast along a line of hills in order to cross Mesopotamia and then headed for the Tigris towards a place called Guagamela. Alexander learned from prisoners he had taken on the march that Darius had drawn up an army that was five times larger than his. It was here at Guagamela that Darius was determined to make his stand. Darius had all the advantages offered by the terrain and the size of his force. All that Alexander had in his favour was that his army had already won two battles against the Persians and the morale of his men was unshakeable.

When Alexander reached the Tigris and found no sign of Darius or his army, he rested his men. That evening there was an eclipse of the moon. The men were worried by what it might portend. Alexander told them that his astrologers had assured him that the eclipse meant that he would win a victory within the month.

The army, which had hauled itself across the vast plains in the summer heat and dust, was eager for the marching to stop and for battle to begin. They knew that if they defeated Darius, the riches of Persia, Babylon, Persepolis and Susa lay spread ahead for them to take. They also knew that there would be a chance for them to rest and to regroup.

As the army approached Guagamela, Alexander took a reconnoitring force ahead. As dusk fell, they came on Darius' vast camp spread out below them. Looking down across the plain towards the gleam of the river, Alexander saw the Persian army spread across the land between the river and the foothills beyond.

Alexander and his officers could hear the dull murmur of men's voices and such was their number it sounded like the roar of the sea – thousands of men waiting, huddled around their twinkling cooking fires, taking what rest they could before their encounter in the killing fields the following day.

Parmenion and the other experienced generals remarked that it would be very difficult to defeat an enemy of such strength, protected as it was by the sweep of the river, in daylight. They urged Alexander to attack by night.

"I will not steal my victory," he told them. Some thought he was boasting, but he knew that, above all, he had to be seen to defeat this vastly superior army in daylight so that they could make no excuses for defeat. When morning came the two armies were seven miles apart. The land in front of the Persian cavalry and scythed chariots had been smoothed clear of any obstacles that might prevent a cavalry charge at speed. Chariots were unstable at the best of times and the Persians had taken no chances – Darius was determined that Alexander should confront the full force of his army.

Alexander and his commanders had reconnoitred the battlefield and decided that when they attacked they would swing the line of battle away from the cleared area in order to give the enemy cavalry and chariots as little chance as possible.

Alexander dressed for the battle in a tunic made in Sicily which was belted round his waist and over a thickly quilted linen corselet which had been captured at Issus. His helmet, the work of Theophilus, was made of steel, which gleamed like polished silver, and was fitted with a steel gorget containing precious stones. His sword, a gift from the King of Citium, was a marvel of lightness and tempering. It was his principal weapon in hand-to-hand fighting. He also wore a cloak which was more ornate than the rest of his armour. It had been made by Helicon, an artist of earlier times, and had been presented to Alexander as a mark of honour by the city of Rhodes. While he was drawing up the phalanx, reviewing the troops or giving out orders, he rode another horse to spare Bucephalus, who was now past his prime. He would mount Bucephalus when the attack finally got under way.

Darius' huge army of Persians, Sogdians, Bactrians, Indian tribesmen, Sythians, Arachotians, Medes, Parthians and many others numbered 40,000 cavalry and one million infantry according to Arrian. Others suggest the more accurate figures might be 34,000 cavalry and 200,000 infantry. Whatever the truth, the Persians vastly outnumbered Alexander's advancing army.

Alexander rode out in front of his men and reminded them that they had come a long way with him. He assured them that they were the best army in the world and that they had no need to fear defeat. He reminded them how far he and his father had brought them from their days as poverty-stricken shepherds and farmers. Now they had vast amounts of loot in the baggage train and were rich men. There was no need to tell them to be brave … they knew that in their hearts. He only asked them all to do their duty, just as they had done before.

Alexander looked along the lines of men drawn up before him and saw that each of them was eager to be recognized by him. They knew that sometimes before a battle he would greet them individually and they loved him for this.

Then he picked out men by name and reminded the others of the bravery that these individuals had shown in past battles. He made heroes of them all. He urged them to advance in silence until the order to attack was given and then to roar out their battle cry to the gods and strike fear into their enemy's hearts. He declared: "If each of you attend to your duty then we shall win. If any man neglect that duty … then the whole army could be in peril."

He raised his right hand and called upon the gods saying that if he were really the son of Zeus then they would surely protect the Greeks. Aristander, the diviner and seer, dressed in a white robe and gold helmet, rode along the ranks and pointed into the early morning sky. There was an eagle circling in the sky above Alexander's head which then turned and flew straight towards the enemy.

Alexander's hand flashed down and the phalanx roared like a flood after the eagle. Alexander made straight for the tall figure of Darius in his chariot who was closely guarded by horsemen. The battle quickly turned from being the fluid charge and countercharge of chariots and cavalry as the infantrymen engaged in vicious hand-to-hand fighting.

At one stage it looked as if the Persians were gaining the upper hand, but Alexander turned his cavalry onto the Persian infantry and this attack from the rear and the efforts of the Greek infantry as they hacked their way clear was enough to send the Persian infantry into panic. The Thessalian cavalry were magnificent against the Persian right flank.

As the general of the Thessalian calvalry, Parmenion needed help to beat off a fierce attack and again Alexander offered the support the older man needed. Shoving their lances into the faces of the Persians and Sythians, the infantry, tight in close order and pikes bristling from

ABOVE *Dressed in all his finery, Alexander the Great and his army faced Darius and the Persian army at the bloody Battle of Guagamela, 331BC.*

their ranks, moved steadily, inexorably forward and it did not take long for Alexander's army to break the Persians.

Darius watched the carnage about him, lost his nerve, turned his chariot and left the battlefield, leaving his men leaderless.

Alexander set off in hot pursuit for as long as daylight remained. Hundreds of Persian stragglers were slaughtered as they ran. Alexander stopped the pursuit and rested his men until midnight, while Parmenion took over the Persian camp and all it contained … baggage, gold, elephants and camels.

At midnight Alexander pressed on to try to catch Darius. While he was still free, Alexander knew that Darius would make trouble. The focus of the next few weeks' campaigning would be to find and capture Darius.

Darius believed that the temptation to head south for Babylon would be too much for Alexander to resist. So he fled into the Armenian mountains and recruited a few thousand mercenary troops to add to his royal guard as he went.

WHAT DID THEY FIND IN BABYLON?

Darius was right. As the army moved, in full battle order, down the Royal Road to Babylon, they passed through a land full of riches. Grain grew in the well-tended fields, a canal system irrigated the land and the date palms providing not only fruit, but which were also woven into material, fermented as liquor or used as firewood. Cattle grazed in the meadows alongside the river and in the estates owned by the royal family or subjects who had been rewarded in the past for services to the throne.

The Macedonians admired the many flocks of game birds and the herds of fine horses. Here were rich villages that paid taxes to the royal family either in kind or in gold.

The huge mud walls of Babylon loomed up from the land. Terraces of trees and shrubs cascaded down the hillsides, flowers bloomed in profusion in these hanging gardens.

The satrap of Babylon, Mazaeus, danced attendance on Alexander and welcomed him as a Babylonian and not as a Persian official. He was married to a Babylonian and perhaps he felt it let him shift his loyalties. Babylon had previously been conquered by the Persians and their temples and gods had been defiled – they could perhaps rightly claim Alexander as their saviour.

Mazaeus encouraged the priests, magistrates and people who opened their city to Alexander to place all their treasures into his hands. In response to their open-handedness, Alexander ordered that the temples destroyed by Xerxes should be rebuilt. The priests were more than delighted when he also took their advice on how to offer sacrifice to the God Bel.

Alexander was shown the vast treasury and annexed it immediately. His army was given a bonus – the equivalent of nearly a year's wages. They would be given time to spend it on women, drink and other pleasures that the sophisticated city offered.

The streets were wide and lined with mud-built, square, windowless, cool buildings. The main temple was vast, as were the great gardens around the city walls. Water was brought into the city by means of a stone viaduct, which also provided water for the city's wondrous gardens.

The Macedonian soldiers remained in Babylon for five months while Alexander planned their next move to the royal city of Susa. Before he left Babylon he appointed Mazaeus as its governor, making it clear that any satrap who played into his hands might well be rewarded and not punished.

In this way Alexander kept men in place who understood how the local systems worked. All they had to do was to keep the peace, act fairly and channel the taxes to him and not to Darius.

Meanwhile back in Greece, Sparta was stirring up trouble and Antipater had his hands full with the revolt until allies from the other city-states threw in their lot with him. Athens and Thebes feared and hated Sparta more than they did Alexander. Macedonia and the city-states settled back into an uneasy truce.

In December 331BC, Alexander led the army, apart from the garrison he left behind in Babylon, along the Royal Road to Susa, which was built on an outcrop of rock overlooking the Kerkha River at the edge of the Zagros Mountains and the Assyrian plains.

Susa was a royal treasure chest. Vast amounts of purple-dyed cloth, piles of gold and precious stones, wonderfully worked Sythian goblets and diadems, magnificent plates and superbly decorated temples and palaces lay in the city. It was here that Alexander left the mother and children of Darius and ordered that they were to be taught Greek.

It was also in Susa that Alexander began to put into practice the dream he had of ignoring the racial and national differences between people and began to try to create a truly united population. He believed that all differences between races could be settled through intermarriage and for that reason encouraged his soldiers to marry local girls and rewarded those who did so with money and grants of land.

Only now could he regard himself as King of Asia ... But there was always the niggling concern that Darius might be plotting trouble out in the vast hinterland of deep mountain valleys and high, eagle-ringed passes to the north. While Alexander relied on all the information his patrols might bring in, it was impossible to establish exactly where Darius was rebuilding his shattered army, or indeed if he was being kept alive by others to use as a pawn in any future dealings with Alexander. Darius was an ever-present threat to the stability of the conquered Persians.

In the spring of 330BC, Alexander knew that before dealing with Darius he had to capture Persepolis, the central focus of the Persian Empire. It lay on the other side of the Zagros Mountains, at the edge of a vast, desolate plain between Isfahan and the ring of mountains that were strung from Armenia and the Caspian Sea in the north to the deserts of the Persian Gulf to the south. Persepolis lay beyond the pass known as the Persian Gates on the edge of the Desert of Lut. Across that desert lay the route to Bactria and the high passes of the Hindu Kush and India.

Persepolis was a magnificent city of palaces and temples. Its approaches were protected not only by warring tribesmen but also by a force of 20,000 soldiers, led by a Persian satrap, who blocked the narrow pass at the Persian Gates. Alexander brushed aside the tribesmen and then marched towards the pass.

He had taken some prisoners on the journey and learned that it was possible to take a contingent of his toughest men over the mountains and round the pass. He would be able to drop down behind the Persian force and, with precise planning between the advance party and the men he had left confronting the Persian Gates, he could engage the Persians in a crushing movement with simultaneous pressure from both front and rear.

He led the advance party over the mountains, by night through snow and sleeting rain. It was a savage forced march, but the Macedonian troops rose to the challenge. Once in position, a trumpet call alerted the army in front of the pass and the Persian force was attacked simultaneously from front and back.

There was no escape for the 20,000 guardians of the pass and the bloodshed was an example of just how ruthless Alexander was prepared to be.

He wanted to get to Persepolis before it was burned to the ground or before the treasures it held were looted either by its citizens or by the men of the Persian army who were still there.

BELOW *Temples and palaces in the ancient city of Persepolis. The city lay beyond the Persian Gates and was the central focus of the Persian Empire.*

RIGHT *Xerxes' Gatehouse in the city of Persepolis.*

He knew that unless he defeated the force at the Persian Gates he was leaving his line of march vulnerable to an attack from behind.

He marched fast from the Persian Gates, leaving the dead where they lay. From the narrow pass the route led out into a bowl in the mountains and on to Persepolis.

Alexander did not reach Persepolis in time to prevent his men from pulling down a huge statue of Xerxes, the Persian hero-king. Alexander debated, on seeing it, whether he would have it raised again or leave it as a monument to the defeat of the Persian Empire. He left the statue where it lay. He wanted to avenge the wrongs he claimed Xerxes had done to the Greek people 200 years before.

WHAT DID THEY
FIND IN PERSEPOLIS?

OPPOSITE *The stairway leading to the Royal Palace in the city for kings and gods – Persepolis.*

In the distance across the rust-coloured earth, the snow-capped mountains lay purple in the heat haze. Imagine a city of wide, low steps and towering over them mighty stone pillars, painted or intricately carved and cut with images of soldiers, guards and horned bulls. Imagine precisely cut pediments and long slabs of wall carved and etched with processions of magi and courtiers.

Water ran through canals cut into the rock, vast stone monuments were carved and painted with images of Darius the Great and his court. Here was a city for kings and for gods.

Priests and nobles thronged the streets in the shade of the buildings as the sun beat out of

RIGHT *From the Hall of One Hundred Columns in the ancient city of Persepolis. A bas-relief of a procession and an audience with King Xerxes.*

the pale blue sky. Envoys from many lands brought tributes to the king, practices which over the years had been memorialized by craftsmen who carved images of such events into the faces of temples and palaces.

Here in the shade of the narrow streets behind the public façade, Sythian goldsmiths tapped delicate patterns into sheets of glowing gold. Dyers and weavers trod on raw wool up to their thighs in the stinking, multi-coloured vats of colour, hung up swathes of wool which would be used to make miraculous carpets – potters and carvers, woodworkers and stonemasons clattered and hammered and made the artefacts for which the city was famed. To be king of all this … this was what it meant to be royal.

It is said that it took 2,000 pairs of mules and 500 camels to carry away the furniture and other treasures Alexander found in Persepolis.

A BRIEF PAUSE

Ten years before, Demaratus, an old friend of Alexander's father, had brought Alexander back from exile. Now he was delighted and wept to see the young king seated on the throne once occupied by the mighty King of Persia, Cyrus the Great, and then by Darius.

Alexander rested his army in the city of Persepolis for five months. However, he could not stay still. Even as winter came down to bring a close on the fighting season, he took men up into the tribal areas of Fars and subdued tribes who had never expected him to wage war in the terrible conditions winter brought to their mountain homes. It was said that if the ice and snow blocked his way he would be the first to get off his horse and hack a path through. Here was a leader who led by example and not by words. Alexander was a leader who refused to rest on his laurels or be shaken.

MAY 330 BC

Alexander then returned to Persepolis to plan his next move to capture Darius and remove the lingering threat that he still posed. It was during this time that the magnificent palace built by Xerxes was burned to the ground and looted.

Some say Alexander chose to burn the palace deliberately to prove he had totally defeated the old regime and that he was determined to extinguish the memory of the old king. Parmenion was said to be against burning the magnificent building on the grounds that it was folly to destroy something that Alexander already owned.

Others say that the palace was set alight by accident or that it happened as a result of an orgy of drinking when the Athenian mistress of Ptolemy, Thais, urged them to burn it down. The story has it that Alexander, drunk, took up a burning torch and the party went reeling off into the night. They arrived at the palace and other Macedonians joined the garlanded Alexander and brought torches too.

They hoped that burning the palace was a sign that he was thinking of turning for home. The magnificent building was razed to the ground, but Alexander was not yet turning his thoughts to Macedonia.

He did, however, arrange for some of his older soldiers and the wounded to return home. He gave them generous pensions and ensured that they would be treated well when they returned to their homeland. He gave vast gifts and valuable pieces of land to his commanders and so bound them to him by his generosity.

When his mother, Olympias, heard of Alexander's great generosity, she urged him not to give too many presents to his friends. Olympias felt that this kind of behaviour would cause jealousy amongst those he ignored.

Alexander was generous to a fault and if anyone asked for help he gave it. On the other hand, if people did not ask or if they had too much pride to ask then they got nothing. Everyone knew where they stood.

There is a story that Alexander used to play a ball game with a group of friends. When one proud young man got the ball he refused to throw it to his king. Eventually Alexander asked the young man why and he answered: "Because you never ask for it."

There was a brief pause as the other players wondered how Alexander would react. Alexander burst out laughing and piled gifts on the young man.

Before he moved off in search of Darius, Alexander had regrouped the army and ensured that it was more mobile. He broke it up into four divisions so that it could cover vast amounts of territory without having to be controlled from the centre. In the vast landmass of mountains, deserts and jealously held tribal lands which he now proposed to control, this was essential. In such terrain war would be more of a guerrilla campaign than the set-piece battles that had defined the campaign to date.

With the coming of spring and with it the approach of the season of war, Alexander worried that his soldiers were becoming soft. They had been enjoying the Sybaritic life they led in Persepolis a little too much. There was food and wine and women, warmth and shelter and the soft life that Alexander knew could be the ruin of a fighting army. Luxury is the true enemy of military might.

At one time Alexander said: "The perfect result of any conquest is that the conquerors avoid doing the same things as the conquered have done." Yet, while living in Persepolis, his army were beginning to live in exactly the same way as the Persians had done. Alexander was more determined than ever to hone his army into a tempered weapon once again.

It was time to find Darius and eliminate him. It was time again for war.

CHAPTER EIGHT

PLOTS, MURDER AND MARRIAGE

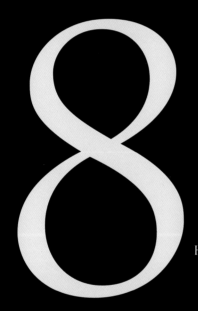

SINCE CROSSING THE HELLESPONT IN MAY 334BC, THE MACEDONIAN ARMY HAD BEEN ON THE MARCH FOR FIVE YEARS. THE MONTHS DURING WHICH IT HAD RESTED IN PERSEPOLIS HAD BEEN A TIME FOR REORGANIZATION AND FOR STRENGTHENING THE GARRISONS LEFT ALONG THE LINE OF ADVANCE THUS FAR.

WHILE THE ARMY RESTED IN PERSEPOLIS, ALEXANDER ALSO CONCENTRATED ON PAYING OFF SOME OF THE LONGER SERVING SOLDIERS AND SENDING THEM HOME WITH SUBSTANTIAL BONUSES. HE ALSO ENCOURAGED OTHER SOLDIERS TO MARRY LOCAL WOMEN IN A BID TO SECURE PERSEPOLIS' ALLEGIANCE TO MACEDONIAN RULE.

ALEXANDER HAD, WHEREVER POSSIBLE, LEFT IN PLACE THE FAMILIAR SYSTEMS OF GOVERNMENT AT LOCAL LEVEL, WHICH WERE ACCEPTABLE TO THE PEOPLE – HE KNEW THAT DRACONIAN MEASURES WOULD ONLY ENSURE UNREST IN THE FUTURE.

ALEXANDER HAD EXPERIMENTED WITH BREAKING UP THE ARMY INTO FAST REACTION FORCES WHICH WERE SMALL AND VERY MANOEUVRABLE. THESE WORKED UNDER INDIVIDUAL COMMANDERS AND WERE VERY SUCCESSFUL IN COMBATING THE TRIBES IN THE MOUNTAINS TO THE NORTH IN PARTHIA AND IN THE ZAGROS MOUNTAINS THAT BORDERED THE CENTRAL PLAIN TO THE WEST, WHERE THE PEOPLE REFUSED TO ACCEPT ALEXANDER AS THEIR KING, JUST AS THEY HAD REFUSED TO ACCEPT DARIUS BEFORE HIM.

This time may also have been a time for reflection. Since the age of 16, when he took the throne, Alexander had been involved in war. For the past five years he had been leading the most successful military campaign and the longest march ever made by an army into Asia.

He had organized the movement of as many as 100,000 men from the mountains of Macedonia to the capital of the Persian Empire – one of the most powerful empires ever known – and they had been fighting all the way.

Alexander had been responsible for ensuring that the army was fed and watered, that its supply lines were protected, that medical care was available, that animals were looked after, that discipline was kept and that his commanders were as focused as he was on the immediate objective. To have

ABOVE *A nineteenth-century engraving showing Persian soldiers charging into battle.*

talked to the men of conquering the world, of marching to the edge of their known world, would perhaps have led to mutiny, but Alexander rode his luck and while he was advancing through the land almost non-stop, no one had either the time or the courage to question what was happening.

Alexander knew the value of personal publicity very well. He was eager to be seen as a man who knew his men and loved them for what they were.

ALEXANDER'S CHARACTER

Over the years the soldiers saw Alexander as a talisman and, as they pressed deeper and deeper into Asia, further and further away from their known world, most of them believed that they relied on him, not only to lead them forward, but also to lead them back home.

Their need for him was brought home to them when he was wounded and suffering from dysentery. He knew there were already some mutterings of unrest, so he took the opportunity to seclude himself from the army.

It was true that the longest serving of them, the Macedonians, were beginning to whisper that they had had enough. Alexander knew that by deliberately remaining out of their sight he would make them uneasy. "What happens if he dies?" "How do we get out of here and back home?" "Who will lead the way?"

He also knew they were jealous of the favours they felt he showed to the Persians who had agreed to fight in his army and to the native leaders he left in power.

When he was persuaded to let his men see him, their unease died down and the whispers about mutiny were silenced. For the moment.

If individuals needed help he was often more than generous. When he decided to send back the older soldiers, some of whom who had been fighting for his father Philip for many years in Macedonia, he made sure that each of them had a share of loot that would set them up on their return.

He knew that many of his men had spent all their money on gambling, women and drink during the army's stay in Persepolis and he knew that many had incurred huge debts. If not dealt with firmly these could lead to disciplinary problems amongst his men in the future. He ordered that all men who had incurred such debts or who had IOUs from other soldiers should report to their senior officers and that their financial problems would be resolved.

ABOVE *The desert beyond Persepolis through which Alexander's army must have marched.*

OPPOSITE *The steady advance of the Macedonian phalanx which was brought to perfection by Alexander the Great who divided the phalanx into units.*

At first the men were suspicious and few of them applied for the money, but they were eventually persuaded to do so and some money from the loot of Persepolis was disbursed to the soldiers to relieve their debts. It may have cost Alexander thousands of talents of silver, but at a stroke Alexander had prevented things from getting out of hand.

An example of his pure generosity happened when an artist, travelling with the army, had been painting the portrait of a lovely young woman. She was a courtesan and was being sent back to Macedonia with the repatriated soldiers. The artist could not stand being parted from her and pretended to be ill so that he might go back with the same group.

Alexander discovered what had happened and the artist was brought in front of him and charged with desertion. When Alexander asked him why, he told him that he had fallen in love with the girl he had been painting and he was desperate to be with her.

Alexander made some enquiries and discovered that the girl was a freeborn Greek courtesan. He told the artist that if he was to win the girl it had to be by love and not coercion.

LEGENDS

Plutarch wrote: "Alexander's reputation for generosity increased with his extraordinary acquisitions. He also had a gracious manner, which is the only thing that gives generosity an irresistible charm."

Ariston, who commanded the Phaeonians, having killed one of the enemy and cut off his head, laid it at Alexander's feet, and said: "Among us, sir, such a gift is rewarded with a golden cup." King Alexander answered with a smile: "An empty one, I suppose. I will give you one full of good wine. Here, my boy, I drink to you."

Or another: One day a poor Macedonian foot soldier was driving a mule loaded down with the king's gold. The mule was exhausted and the man took the load onto his own shoulders and carried it, tottering on his way. He was almost defeated by the weight on his back when Alexander saw him. He asked what was in the load and was told. He went to the worn-out man and called to him. "Hold on, friend, the rest of the way and then carry it to your tent. It is all yours."

And yet another: There was an occasion when Alexander was leading a patrol searching the edge of the desert for a rebel called Spitamenes. Alexander and his men were desperate for water. They came on a small group of native people who were walking towards their village in what shade they could find. They had a little brackish water in an earthen jar.

The story goes that when they saw it was Alexander, they poured their precious water into his helmet. He asked them where they were taking it. They said it was for their children, but that they could always beget new children so Alexander was welcome to drink.

Alexander lifted the helmet to his mouth and then looked round at the squadron of soldiers with him and gently poured the helmet full of water back into the earthen jug held by the man who had offered it to him. There was not nearly enough for his men and if they could not have water then neither would he. It is no wonder his soldiers were willing to follow him to the end of their known world.

He freed the young artist and urged him to court the young woman as he would any other freeborn woman and if he could win her, then no one would be happier than Alexander.

By this time Darius was a captive in the hands of his cousin, Bessus. He was still alive because Bessus and others thought he would be a useful bargaining tool, if they ever needed one, should Alexander catch up with them.

Alexander had decided that the time to begin the serious search for Darius had come and he sent out spies to search for news. He also began to make personal efforts to regain complete fitness. He had to set an example to his less-than-battle-hardened warriors.

He began by warning his officers that they were endangering their men and themselves by aping the lifestyle of those they had defeated. They must pull themselves together and join him in a regime that would make them ready for the campaign to capture Darius.

The officers were not happy and began to mutter about his being too proud, too high and mighty. They believed he was even beginning to believe what others said of him – that he was divine.

It was true that having adopted the ceremonial dress of the Persians, Alexander had also begun to adopt some of their customs. One, in particular, caused the Macedonian officers and men considerable anger. "Proskynesis" was the custom of bowing very low before approaching the king or being allowed to kiss his cheek in greeting.

It was more than freeborn Macedonian men were willing to tolerate, but it was accepted by the Persian mercenaries and other members of the army. No Macedonian, however, would bow down before speaking to his king.

Maybe Alexander had forgotten that kings in Macedonia were proclaimed not necessarily by inheritance and that what can be proclaimed can equally well be dismissed by proclamation.

Trying to introduce what was a Persian custom of obeisance to those surrounding him was not a wise thing to have done and it led to the first inkling that there were men willing to defy him. It would ultimately lead to one of the greatest tragedies of his life.

For the moment, he tried to set the army an example by taking strenuous exercise. He hunted the fiercest animals and took great personal risks. Maybe he hoped this would shame his army into action.

In late spring 330BC he left Persepolis in pursuit of Darius. Both Plutarch and Arrian describe the ensuing campaign in detail.

Many of Darius' men had deserted him as he retreated and some surrendered to Alexander. Two of these deserters, Bagistanes, a Babylonian nobleman, and Antibels asked to see Alexander who was campaigning with his cavalry.

The deserters told him that Darius had been put under arrest by his cousin, Bessus, in collusion with Barsaentes and Nabarzanes. Despite the fact that Alexander and his horsemen were tired and hungry, he immediately set out with his cavalry companions and the toughest light infantry.

Marching day and night they stopped at noon for a brief rest, and after a second all-night march came to the camp that Bagistanes had informed him of. Darius was not there.

Alexander pushed his men hard, even though they were exhausted, as they raced in final pursuit of Darius. They learned from some local people of a short cut across uninhabited country and took it. Alexander dismounted 500 cavalrymen and mounted up his toughest infantrymen and on they went ahead of the rest of the infantry, as a flying column.

They covered 50 miles (80 kilometres) in one night. Plutarch records that the group covered 400 miles (644 kilometres) in 11 days. This crippling pace killed some of the horses and exhausted the men. They came on Persian stragglers from the force surrounding the fleeing Darius. These stragglers either ran for the hills or turned to fight desperately and died for their pains. On the cavalry swept north towards the Caspian Gates between the mountains that led down to the Caspian shore.

Through cruel and arid land, through mud-built villages, past tall palms at small springs, the dust from their racing hooves billowed low across the earth.

Eventually, the leading 60 soldiers in the group rode through a ramshackle village. They passed wagons filled with women and children, gold plate and jewels and learned that Darius was being carried in a covered cart, that his cousin Bessus and the others were moving as fast as they could to keep ahead of Alexander. They were not more than an hour ahead.

The cavalry came upon an abandoned wagon. In the wagon, under a filthy and bloody blanket, a Macedonian named Polystratus found Darius riddled with javelins, lying in his own blood. Polystratus looked upon Darius and pitied him. Once this man had been the most powerful of kings and now he was reduced to begging for water. Polystratus gave him some from his flask.

As Darius drank the cold water he looked up at the Macedonian soldier and said: "Friend, this fills the measure of my misfortune, to think that I am not able to reward you for this act of kindness. But Alexander will not let you go without reward and the gods will reward Alexander for his humanity to my mother, to my wife and children. Tell him I gave him my hand, for I give it to you in his place."

Darius took the hand of the Macedonian cavalryman and died.

Alexander came up to the cavalry unit too late to speak with Darius. He looked down at the dead man, closed his eyes and laid his own cloak over the body. He ordered that the body be sent back to Darius' mother in Susa so that it might be given royal burial as was proper.

The hunt for Bessus, the killer, who had dared not only to murder his king but also to take his title, was successful. After he had been found guilty of regicide, Alexander ordered that

ABOVE *The soldiers of Alexander's army took every chance to compete in games. They often used them as a form of exercise.*

Bessus be scourged and then executed.

He was put between two tall trees. The tops of the trees were drawn down and one leg and one arm were tied to each tree. When the ropes tethering the tree tops were cut they sprang powerfully upright tearing Bessus in two.

During the campaign to capture Darius various mercenary troops from the Persian army came over to Alexander and, when they reached Zadracarta, south of the Caspian Sea, they were also reinforced by a division of new recruits, led by Craterus.

Greek mercenaries from the routed Persian army asked to come over, but Alexander refused to guarantee them safe conduct as they had fought against Greeks.

While he rested his troops for 15 days at Zadracarta, sacrifices were made to the gods, games were celebrated and then he moved on across the river Ochus towards Bactria, where he was visited by Satibarzanes, the satrap of the province. Alexander confirmed that he was to stay in office and was rewarded when the satrap, a few months later, fomented revolution against Alexander's rule.

Satibarzanes was astonished by the speed of Alexander's reaction. Covering 75 miles (121 kilometres) in mountain country, in two days, Alexander did not catch the rebel leader but sold into slavery, or had killed, anyone who had supported him.

It was during the campaign against Satibarzanes that Alexander was hit in the knee by a Persian arrow that shattered the bone – pieces of which had to be picked out of the wound before it could heal. He was also suffering from dysentery at the time, but somehow still managed to go on with the campaign.

Alexander was becoming anxious as to whether the Macedonians might refuse to follow him further. The going was hard, they were many months' march from home and some of them had now been away for more than five years.

In October 330BC, news of a plot reached Alexander's ears. It was a plot that was led by an old and trusted friend and Alexander did not want to believe it.

There were few men as important to Alexander as Philotas, who commanded the companion cavalry. He was son of Parmenion, the old general and friend of Alexander's father. Yet the son was implicated in a plot. He was a kindly man, but rather loud and uncouth. Even his father had warned him not to get above himself. "Be less, my son. Be less."

Alexander could not believe that a man on whom he had bestowed honours and trust could

be involved in a plot to remove him.

Philotas had been suspected of treasonous activities when Damascus was taken. A girl was handed over to him and he made her his mistress. It seems he boasted to her that Alexander was nothing and that his whole reputation was built on the work he, Philotas, and his father had done. The mistress was a Greek girl called Antigone.

She repeated what her lover had told her to a friend who passed on the remarks and the words eventually reached Craterus who, with Hephaestion, was a pillar of the High Command. The girl was ordered to continue to listen and to report back. Alexander was a patient man. He waited and listened and waited…

Meanwhile a group of young men, the Pages, had also begun a plot to kill Alexander in his sleep. One of these young men had dared to race in front of Alexander during a hunt and had been whipped for it. This angered the Pages and other junior officers worked on their anger to bring about Alexander's death.

News of this plot was brought to Philotas, but the men with the information were refused access to Alexander twice by Philotas. When Alexander heard this and that one of the suspects had died resisting arrest, he had Philotas arrested and tortured in front of the most powerful officers of the court. It would act as a deterrent to others with similar ambitions.

Plutarch wrote: "Alexander placed himself behind a tapestry to hear the examination. When he heard Philotas bemoaning himself in such a lamentable manner, and had recourse to such mean supplications to Hephaestion, he is reported to have said, 'Oh Philotas, how dare you with such unmanly weakness take part in such a great and dangerous enterprise?'"

Philotas was executed and immediately a fast rider rode post haste to Media, where Parmenion, father of Philotas, was commanding a section of the army. A written order, under the seal of Alexander, was handed to one of the aides-de-camp who opened an order to execute

Parmenion. Parmenion was slaughtered instantly.

Alexander was now aware of several plots against him and was justifiably eager to stamp them out. He did it with ruthless ferocity. By the mores of his time he was acting quite correctly and with great political skill. If he had not had the father killed there might well have been a blood feud between them and, as Parmenion commanded a large part of Alexander's army, it would have been a potential danger to Alexander's security had he not acted.

The army marched north through Bactra, across the Oxus and to Sogdiana, then back towards Alexander's next main goal … Afghanistan and India.

It was at this time that Alexander heard that Calisthenes, the army's travelling historian, was asked by a young officer what it was necessary to do in order to become the most famous of men. He also heard the reply: "You become famous by killing the most famous of men."

As a result of this, and of reports that Calisthenes was involved in the Pages' plot, he found himself in prison where he was held until he died, it was said, "of corpulence and lice."

However, it was the cold-blooded, political execution of a respected and experienced general like Parmenion that made so many of his senior subordinates fear Alexander.

In the spring of 329BC, Alexander led his army towards the Hindu Kush. At the same time, detachments were in pursuit of Spitamenes who, the previous summer, had destroyed a Macedonian force at Maracanda (Samarkand).

The campaign against the charismatic Spitamenes was a classic mountain attack with hit-and-run raids by his army against detachments of Alexander's army. Spitamenes' force was gradually reduced by death and desertion, but he refused to give in, even though his fellow rebels felt that they were about to fall to the inexorable forces that Alexander had sent against them.

Coenus, one of the generals Alexander trusted with this campaign, confronted Spitamenes' cavalry and in the ensuing battle put them to flight. It was the last straw for the Sythians and the Bactrians who were fighting alongside Spitamenes.

They deserted and, at the same time, a third tribal force, the Massagetae, plundered Spitamenes' baggage train and took him prisoner as they headed off into the desert. Coenus reported to Alexander that the threat from Spitamenes was over. His head was sent to Coenus' camp in a gesture that the rebellious Massagetae hoped would ensure that they were left alone.

In the autumn of 328BC, Alexander was involved in cold-blooded murder. He was in Marakanda (Samarkand) in the mountains beyond the Oxus and north of the Hindu Kush, many months' march from Macedonia.

A delegation of men arrived in the camp with a present of fresh Greek fruit for the king. He admired the ripe fruit and sent for Cleitus, one of his oldest and best friends. Cleitus was almost equal in favour with Hephaestion because he had saved Alexander's life at Granicus, in the early days of the campaign.

Cleitus was sacrificing three sheep to the gods when Alexander sent for him. He immediately left the ceremony and went to his king. The sheep had been completely prepared and libations had been poured over them. They followed him into Alexander's tent and Alexander was concerned enough to asked Aristander, his diviner, and Cleomantis the Spartan, what this might mean. Both felt it was an evil omen, so Alexander immediately ordered that sacrifice be made for Cleitus' safety.

Alexander was still disturbed because a few days before he had had a dream in which he saw Cleitus sitting with the sons of Parmenion dressed in black and all four of them dead. Now Parmenion and his sons were dead. One son dead in battle, one son executed and Parmenion murdered on Alexander's orders. It was an unsettling vision for a religious man like Alexander.

Cleitus and Alexander sat down together with others and began to eat and drink. As the drink took hold, one of them began to sing a song that mocked some Macedonian commanders who had recently been defeated by Spitamenes. The older Macedonians took exception to the song and the singer, but Alexander ordered the singer to sing on as he was enjoying it.

This was at a time when Alexander had adopted the habits of dress and court etiquette of the Persian court and now to hear these foreign soldiers mocking them made the Macedonian officers angry.

Cleitus was a rough, tough soldier; he had had a great deal to drink and he shouted out angrily that it was insulting to Macedonians and that it was not right that this should happen in front of barbarians and enemies. The generals in question might have been unlucky, but they were still better men than those around the room who were laughing at them.

"You would dress their cowardice in the softer name of misfortune would you?" retorted Alexander. "You must be talking about yourself."

Cleitus jumped to his feet and shouted at the king: "Yes, it was my cowardice that saved you. You, who claim to be descended from the gods, when you had your back to Spithridates' sword. It is by the blood of the Macedonians and their wounds that you have grown so great that you refuse to acknowledge Philip as your father, and need to pass yourself off as the son of Ammon."

Alexander was furious: "You scum, do you think you can keep on talking about me like this? You talk like this and stir up the Macedonians to mutiny. Do not think you can enjoy it for long."

Alexander looked around the room and saw the Persian courtiers and the other foreign generals drinking at his table watching him. No doubt Cleitus saw them too and it only inflamed his anger.

"What do we enjoy now?" said Cleitus. "What reward do we have for all our work? We envy those who did not live to see Macedonians bleed under barbarian rods, or beg Persians for access to their king."

All around the older men were trying to calm things down, but Alexander's new young friends began to abuse Cleitus as less than Greek and a barbarian himself. Cleitus refused to back down now.

"Go on, say what you have to say or do not ask freeborn men to your table who will speak their minds. Perhaps it were better to pass your life with barbarians and slaves who will worship your Persian belt and white robe without a thought? Leave free men alone."

Alexander hurled the first thing he could lay his hands on at Cleitus to silence him. It was an apple. Then he reached for his dagger, but one of his bodyguards, Aristophanes, had moved it out of harm's way, which alarmed Alexander. Men gathered around Cleitus and begged him to be quiet.

Alexander leapt to his feet and called out in Macedonian for his bodyguard, which was a sign of extreme emergency. He ordered his trumpeter to sound the alarm and because the trumpeter was unwilling to obey, he struck him with his fist. Cleitus' friends had, by now, hustled him out of the banqueting room and for a moment things calmed down.

Then, almost comically, Cleitus came in at another door and recited in a loud and contemptuous voice a line from Euripides' play Andromichae:

"Alas, what evil customs reign in Greece
Shall one man claim the trophies won by thousands?"

Then Alexander snatched a spear from one of his guards, turned and ran Cleitus through. Cleitus fell with a roar of pain and died. The king was no longer angry and pulled the spear from the body and would, according to Plutarch, have plunged it into his own throat if his guards had not seized him and carried him to his chamber.

Arrian writes: "Cleitus deserves the severest censure for his bitter accusations to his king, so I cannot but be sorry for Alexander who had apparently shown himself capable of the two greatest vices in life … uncontrolled anger and drunkenness … But then he is exceedingly to be praised because the moment his wine left him he was grieved and repented…" The fact is that Alexander had murdered an old and trusted general in a rage.

He did suffer after the killing and went for days without food or drink. Then his friends' advice began to take effect. He had a duty not to allow himself to sink into despair but to rally and lead his men once more.

Anaxarchus, one of the sophists he had brought with him, sat by his bedside as he still lay in despair at what he had done. He advised his king: "… all the actions of so great a king as he was should first appear just to himself and afterwards will be seen to be just by the rest of mankind."

Alexander rallied and, learning that rebel leaders were whipping up unrest amongst the tribes who had only been partly subdued even under the Persian Empire, decided it was time to take them on.

It was winter 327BC, but Alexander did not let snow, ice and storms stop his soldiers in their work. He learned that a number of rebels, including the wife and children of Oxyartres, the Bactrian chieftain who was one of those who refused to submit to Alexander, had gone to the Rock of Sogdiana – a refuge believed to be impregnable.

It was early spring when Alexander advanced to the Rock of Sagdiana. He was very angry. It appears that he had offered them terms to accept defeat. The rebellious tribesmen could go to their homes unhurt if they would give up their stronghold. The answer had been roars of laughter and the suggestion that he should find soldiers with wings to capture the Rock for him. No one else, they believed, could do it.

To make matters even harder for Alexander and his army, there was deep snow on the approaches to the Rock of Sogdiana.

To find his winged soldiers was a challenge thrown down and when Alexander approached the sheer rock he had already offered a prize of 12 talents to the first man up, 11 to the second and so on down to the 12th.

Arrian wrote: "Having chosen out of his whole army about 300 men who in previous sieges had climbed walls and rocks, they took with them small iron tent pegs which they were going to drive into the snow where it was hard enough or into the rock where no snow lay. They tied strong ropes to the pins and in the dead of the night made their way to the steepest part of the rock which would be least well guarded. They began to climb. Thirty fell and died on the rocks or lay buried in the snow where it was impossible to find their bodies. The rest reached the top at daybreak made a signal to their friends below them by waving handkerchiefs to them. The Rock was theirs."

A herald was sent to give the enemy the news that Alexander had found his winged soldiers and that the defenders should look up and see them on the summit of the Rock.

The rebels surrendered for they had no way of knowing how large the force was. The prisoners included many women and children, among them were the wife and daughters of Oxyaertes.

Arrian writes: "One daughter was called Roxana, a virgin, but marriageable and, by general consent of writers, the most beautiful of all Asiatic women, Darius' wife excepted. Nevertheless, Alexander, struck by her beauty, resolved not to offer violence to a captive, he forbore to gratify his desires till he took her, afterwards, to wife."

Plutarch claims that Alexander first saw Roxana, not as a prisoner of war coming down from the sheer rocks on an early spring day in the mountains, but that he saw her dancing at a banquet that was prepared to celebrate the alliance between Alexander and her father. Plutarch tells us that she was the only woman he loved. Maybe. Or maybe it was a marriage of state

ABOVE *A glorified version of the marriage of Roxana, daughter of Oxyartes, to Alexander the Great. Their son was born after Alexander died.*

RIGHT *The prospect of marching through land like this, as he headed towards India, led Alexander to abandon the loot he had taken from the Persians and burn it as an example to his men.*

convenience, like his father's to Olympias.

Whatever the truth, it was remembered even 1,500 years later when Marco Polo wrote about passing through the ruins of a city where legend had it that they met. A city of unkempt orchards of plum trees and wild apples, peaches and pears and blackened walls left by Ghengis Khan when he came with his hordes.

As for Alexander's dream … it was still possible. The army was with him. They had no choice, as they had learned when he lay sick with dysentery and a shattered knee. Alexander knew the men were restless. The Macedonians disliked his closeness to the Persians who had volunteered to fight in his army. Many of them had been on the march for seven years. Alexander knew the men were ripe for mutiny so he lay in his tent nursing his wound and left the army to themselves. They very soon understood that the only one who could lead them home again, when he chose to, was Alexander. The men came and begged to see him. He had them in his control again.

Now, deep in the mountains bordering India and Afghanistan, the army was to move on from its headquarters in Maracanda towards Tashkent, where Alexander had ordered a city to be built and called Alexandria the Furthest.

Here Alexander replaced the original incompetent governor. In Alexandria the Furthest, as in the other towns he had founded on his route, he encouraged the settlement of Greeks in the belief that by so doing he could spread the idea of integration between races.

In the summer of 327BC, Alexander began his advance towards India. He saw his troops were weighed down with their loot and were unable to march. Early in the morning, as they were about to march out, the baggage carts were waiting. Alexander walked down to his own

carts filled with his booty and set fire to all of his treasures. He also burned that of his friends … Orders were given that the men do as he had done.

They did as he ordered and then advanced into the high mountains and through to the terrible pass that led onto the raw and fearful Khyber Pass. There were bursts of colour from the flowers that bloom so briefly in the high hills. Above them in the ice-clear skies the dark, spiralling, gliding shapes of eagles soared and, thousands of feet below the marching army, the river Kumar, a tributary of the Indus that winds through the rocky defiles and gorges.

At best the land is inhospitable – dry winds blast across the dust-strewn hillsides, and through the gorges. On the tracks there is no shade and little water. The tribesmen along the route offered, as they have through history, nothing but hostility, for they guarded their land with passion.

The army was divided into two. Half, under the command of Hephaestion, took the high road through the pass. Men, animals and the baggage train, including women and children, wound up the grit-strewn track, along the side of gorges, curving on the narrow path into the distance and climbing ever higher until even flames on cooking fires would not burn.

Alexander's army of Macedonians, Thessalians, Athenians, Bactrians, Persians, Cretans, Cypriots and Greek mercenaries came to the roof of the world and looked down … down … down across the wrinkled surface of the earth and saw India.

BELOW *The Khyber Pass and the advance into India.*

CHAPTER NINE
INDIA AND THE FINAL BATTLE

9

AFTER TRAVELLING THROUGH THE
KHYBER PASS, ALEXANDER TOOK
THE GUARDS, THE CAVALRY
NOT UNDER THE COMMAND OF
HEPHAESTION, THE ARCHERS AND
THE MOUNTED JAVELIN MEN
ALONG THE COURSE OF THE RIVER
COPHEN. THEY TRAVELLED A ROUGH
AND BROKEN LAND.

ALEXANDER AND HIS MEN CROSSED THE RIVER COPHEN
WITH DIFFICULTY AND, ONCE ACROSS, ALEXANDER MOUNTED HIS 800
MACEDONIAN INFANTRYMEN. NOW HE COULD MOVE WITH SPEED AND
ATTACK ANYONE WHO STOOD IN HIS WAY.

DURING HIS FIRST SERIOUS ENGAGEMENT WITH THE NATIVES
ALEXANDER WAS WOUNDED IN THE SHOULDER BY AN ARROW. THE
BATTLE CONTINUED AND THE NEXT DAY THE MACEDONIANS BROKE
THROUGH THE EARTHWORKS, SLAUGHTERED THE FIGHTING MEN AND
BUTCHERED ALL PRISONERS OUT OF REVENGE FOR THE WOUND THEY
HAD GIVEN TO THEIR KING. THE TOWN WAS RAZED TO THE GROUND.

AS A RESULT OF THIS BUTCHERY MANY OTHER TOWNS ON HIS ARMY'S
ROUTE TOWARDS THE INDUS SURRENDERED WITHOUT FIGHTING.

PTOLEMY AND HIS TROOPS NOW JOINED ALEXANDER. WHEN THE
ARMY CAME OUT OF THE MOUNTAINS AND DOWN TO A SETTLEMENT
CALLED ARIGAEUM ALEXANDER FOUND IT HAD BEEN BURNT BY THE
INHABITANTS AND WAS COMPLETELY ABANDONED. IT WAS HERE THAT
CRATERUS REJOINED ALEXANDER'S ARMY.

Alexander decided that this city stood at a good strategic site and ordered Craterus to fortify it and to settle it with any of the natives who were willing to return to the city. He also settled those of his men who were no longer fit for service or for the hardships of the march. They provided the foundations of a garrison town which would protect his lines of communication.

He moved on from there, setting up pockets of his soldiers in blockhouses along their route to deny the natives free access to the land and to protect his line of retreat should it have become necessary.

At this time a number of cities were being besieged and their rulers came to him asking for terms. They were astonished to find Alexander in his tent, still dirty and unkempt from the battlefield. A cushion was brought for him and he took it and gave it to the most senior of the supplicants, Acouphis, and asked him to be seated. Acouphis was very impressed by this courtesy and asked him what he wanted the people to do to earn his friendship and to lift the siege.

"They must appoint you as their governor and send me 100 of their best men for hostages," said Alexander.

Acouphis laughed and replied: "I shall govern them better, my lord, if you would take the worst instead of the best."

It was at about this time that Alexander performed another astounding military feat.

THE ROCK OF ARNOS

Arrian writes: "There was a report that even Hercules, though the son of Zeus, was not able to take the fortress on this rock. Whether the Theban or the Tyrian or the Egyptian Heracles did, in fact, go to India I cannot affirm as true. I am inclined to believe the contrary, because, whatever is difficult to be accomplished men, to raise the difficulty still the higher, have reported that Hercules attempted it in vain."

Whatever the truth of the legend, Alexander had a problem. The Indians in and around the town of Bazira fled to the Rock of Arnos which was in fact a ridge commanding the river Indus about 75 miles (121 kilometres) north of Attock. The rock stood 7,000 feet (2,134 metres) high, about 25 miles (40 kilometres) in circumference and had only one rock-hewn track to the top. There was plenty of water and woodland and arable land for supplies for the population of Bazira and its surrounding countryside to survive for months.

While Alexander, with Craterus and Ptolemy, besieged the stronghold, he sent Hephaestion in advance down to the Indus with instructions to build a bridge across it.

Alexander, meanwhile, arrived in Embolima close to the Rock and ordered Craterus to lay in all necessary supplies for a long siege in case they could not take the Rock by assault.

He moved to reconnoitre the stronghold with a force of archers, the best armed and fittest infantrymen, 200 mounted archers and 200 companions of the bodyguard.

It was now that he had yet another stroke of good luck. Some local natives surrendered to him and told him they would take him to the most vulnerable part of the rock on the other side of the cliff that faced them.

In order to take the mountain fortress, Alexander decided that Ptolemy should attack from one side and his force from the other. Ptolemy had to advance up narrow and dangerous tracks,

ABOVE *Ptolemy, a great supporter of the plight of the Macedonians, who was to rule in Egypt after Alexander died.*

but was to wait for Alexander's men to get into position before attacking. To achieve this, Alexander had to create a bridge across a deep ravine strong enough to take men and heavy siege engines.

At first the Indian defenders on top of the rock jeered when they saw the army below them making wattle rafts which they threw into the ravine. These they piled up with earth and stones. On top of this they laid more wattle rafts to hold the pile together and piled up more earth and stones. It was backbreaking and terrible work under continuous fire from the arrows of the defenders. Alexander created an earthwork strong enough to support the men and the siege engines to attack the stronghold.

When everything was in place, he and a party of 700 climbed the Rock, hauling each other to the top. In this way he was able to take the Indians from one side while Ptolemy and his force confronted them from the other.

Many of the Indian defenders threw themselves from the cliffs rather than submit. Alexander made a sacrifice on the Rock and garrisoned it with troops commanded by an Indian who had taken service under Alexander some time before.

Alexander was a leader who believed in encouraging his men. He knew fear and understood that most men felt it before committing themselves to battle. It is said that just before an encounter like that at the Rock, Alexander was talking to a nervous young Macedonian soldier who was also called Alexander.

Alexander told him, kindly: "You will have to prove yourself a brave man to live up to your name." The young man fought with great courage and was killed in the battle. It is said that Alexander was very sad at the news.

The army had come through the terrible march across and through the mountains. Their leader was still intent on going forward and taking on almost impossible odds. So far his luck and theirs had held, but for how much longer? The old troopers were tired of the perpetual marching, the never-ending battles and skirmishes. Maybe they were afraid that they had put their lives on the line once too often. Whatever the reason, they were starting to question the future again.

How far? How much further? How long? For how much longer would they go on being led by a general whose ambition would, as far as they could understand it, be limited only by coming to the ocean at the end of the world … Another day … another battle … another death.

Alexander sent messages to Ambhi, the ruler of Taxila, in the area now known as Rawlpindi. He urged Ambhi to meet him and to bring with him other chiefs from the banks of the Indus. Alexander wanted to be able to find a way through this land without opposition. Alexander had learned through spies that Ambhi would be glad of his help against King Porus of Pauravas, whose kingdom threatened his security.

Alexander knew there was a diplomatic deal to be done if Ambhi would meet him. Ambhi came carrying gifts and offered him 25 war elephants to add to his forces. He was a wise man and he and Alexander found that they liked and respected each other.

They sat together in Alexander's tent while the army went through its daily routines – cleaning, mending weapons, caring for the horses, practising their various skills. The clamour of metal on metal, of men laughing and calling to friends, of work parties hauling in fuel, cooking pots steaming, fires with blue smoke rising into the pale sky and behind them the fearsome mountains they had crossed. To get to this point had taken eight years, fighting all the way. These were the men Ambhi knew could defeat his old neighbour and enemy, Porus. The two men sat together and talked.

"What occasion is there for war between us? You are not come to take from us our water or other necessities of life. The only things that reasonable men fight for," said the Indian ruler.

He smiled at the young man sitting in the doorway of the tent always watching his men going about the business of setting up camp and honing their battle skills while he conducted the business of the day.

Ambhi went on: "If I have more gold and silver and other possessions and am richer than you, I am willing to offer you a part. If I have less than you I have no objection to sharing in your bounty."

Alexander turned and took his hand. "If you think that your civil words will let you escape without a conflict you are deceived. I will fight with you to the last. But it shall be in favours and benefits, for you shall not defeat me in generosity."

An alliance was forged between the two men and Alexander moved on into more hostile territory towards the river called Hydaspes.

Indian princes relied on mercenaries to fight for them and, from time to time, these mercenaries caused Alexander to lose many men. When he had overcome one particular town he made a truce with the mercenaries and let them leave. They marched out without their weapons and were instantly put to death by Alexander's soldiers.

Plutarch writes that this was a disgrace to Alexander's reputation as a soldier.

EARLY SUMMER 326BC

Alexander had to defeat Porus if he was to continue on his line of march across India, so he believed he had nothing to lose. The Battle of the Hydaspes was to be a terrible battle.

As the army marched the 100 miles (161 kilometres) from Taxila to the river Hydaspes,

ABOVE *A relief sculpture of elephants and warriors marching into battle.*

Alexander had sent out scouting parties to reconnoitre the line of advance for his army. He knew from them that King Porus, an enemy of Taxila, had placed his army on the eastern bank of the Hydaspes river.

He had a huge force to oppose the advancing Macedonian army. Cavalry, infantry, war chariots and the terrifying spectacle of hundreds of fighting elephants. The numbers depended on who was writing: Arrian, Diodorus or Curtius. Whatever the true figures, a vast force barred the way on the far bank of the Hydaspes, which was already beginning to flood from the monsoon rains. Alexander had little choice – he had to cross the river soon under attack from the far bank or he would have to wait for months.

He knew from his scouts and his own observations that the war elephants guarded the fords across the river and he also knew that the horses, even his faithful Bucephalus, were terrified by the size and trumpeting of these huge animals.

Merely getting his army across the rising river would be a fantastic feat – to do so under continuous attack from the far bank would be almost unthinkable.

Arrian describes the location: "There was a rock on the bank of the Hydaspes where a channel makes a mighty sweep. The rock is covered with trees. At a small distance was an island overrun with woods and uninhabited and fit for his purpose. Considering that his cavalry, as well as the infantry, might be concealed there, he determined to ferry over … The headland and island were 17 miles (27 kilometres) from the enemy camp."

Alexander also observed a deep ditch near the bank in which he could hide the movements of his men, their horses and even their supporting arms. This was to prove crucial in winning the tactical battle, which relied as much on subterfuge and psychology as on force of arms.

Alexander ordered his cavalry to parade at night along the Western bank, making a noise and raising their battle cry from time to time. This he did for several nights and each time Porus marched his elephants up and down the eastern shore to block any attempted crossing. Then he split the army into a number of separate columns and ordered them to march up and down the banks in daylight as if looking for a suitable place to cross.

Then he had corn brought into the main camp from the surrounding country as if he intended to wait until the rains stopped. He had tent skins converted into rafts by stuffing them with hay and kept fires burning at various places along the Western bank at night. Pickets were set up with orders to raise a din and to ensure that the enemy was never sure if an attack was coming or from where it might come.

Secretly, using the wide ditches and the natural hiding places that led to the river, Alexander had brought 30 oared galleys and boats in sections to be ready for the river crossing.

It was essential that Alexander make the crossing with a large enough force to turn one wing of Porus' army. In that way, the centre would have to turn to protect itself and Alexander's army could sweep across the swollen river and attack the now-vulnerable centre.

He embarked his advance force of 5,000 cavalry and 10,000 infantry on a night of storm and thunder. They were safely in their galleys and heading for what they believed was the far bank of the river. They were wrong.

Alexander found himself, his bodyguard and cavalry on a second island separated from the far shore by a wide channel swollen with the rains. As Arrian wrote: "At its shallowest it was over the breast of the foot soldiers and so deep that the horses only keep their heads above the river."

It seemed impossible to cross before Porus moved his army to face them. However, Alexander took the cavalry and infantry across the river onto the far bank, regrouped, skirmished with soldiers from Porus' main army and then advanced six miles (ten kilometres) to engage the enemy.

Porus had to decide if the movement of the boats his scouts had seen on the river beyond the islands was yet another feint. He hesitated too long and this hesitation completely justified Alexander's previous manoeuvres along the river bank. By the time Porus moved, Alexander's force had regrouped and was advancing in battle formation. This was the first of several brilliant tactical successes for Alexander at the Hydaspes.

Porus sent one of his sons with 3,000 cavalry and 120 chariots to oppose Alexander. Alexander destroyed the cavalry, killed Porus' son and captured the chariots which had been forced to stop in the mud near the river bank.

Now was the time for the rest of the army to cross and rejoin Alexander. As they did so, Porus, who was himself a great general and a brave man, drew up his new front. The elephants formed a line in front of the infantry in order to terrify Alexander's cavalry. Behind them were the foot soldiers who extended in wings on both sides – on the flanks of the infantry, more cavalry were stationed behind the war chariots he had left in reserve.

Alexander used the lie of the land skilfully to confuse Porus. He sent a squadron of cavalry under Coenus to work its way, under the cover of the wide ditches, behind and to the right of the enemy.

Alexander's infantry were going to have to confront the centre of Porus' army without the support of the cavalry. To do this, he knew he had to destroy the enemy cavalry, otherwise they would close like the jaws of a pincer on his attacking infantrymen. He had to ensure that all of Porus' cavalry was engaged on one flank only.

PORUS THE KING

Porus was a big man. Some say he was as much as six feet three inches tall (one-point-nine metres) and powerfully built. It is said that when he was mounted on a fighting elephant he looked as an ordinary man looked when seated on a horse.

His elephant was very large and seemed to understand that while his master was fighting strongly it too should defend his master as well as it could. When it realized that Porus was shattered by wounds "it knelt quietly for fear Porus might fall off. With its trunk it took hold of each spear and drew it out of his body."

Even in defeat, Porus was a man of great dignity. When Alexander asked him how he wished to be treated, Porus answered: "As a king."

Alexander said: "I would do that for my own sake. What can I do for yours?"

Porus replied: "My first request compasses all my wishes."

Alexander not only returned his kingdom to him, but also gave him land and villages from the peoples he had already defeated. King Ambhi of Taxila may not have been delighted by the result.

INSET *Alexander meets King Porus of India after defeating him in battle. It was at this time that Bucephalus died.*

This he engineered magnificently. Horse archers engaged the cavalry on the left wing. Then he planned to throw a force of cavalry, that was very obviously too weak to defeat the Indian cavalry, into the attack. Porus, Alexander judged, would be tempted by their obvious weakness and send his cavalry from the right wing to ensure the destruction of Alexander's archers and also his cavalry at the same time. It worked.

As soon as Porus committed his troops, Coenus, observing this from his place of hiding to the rear, was to attack in the flank and rear of the enemy while Alexander charged the front.

And so it happened. Advancing infantrymen had to brave the savagery of the war elephants. Men were tossed aside and broken by the swinging trunks of the animals; others were stamped to a pulp under their huge feet. Slowly, though, the infantrymen got close enough to use axes to hamstring the animals.

The elephants eventually backed away from the advancing phalanx, which by now had linked shields. As they backed they panicked and wheeled and stamped their keepers and the Indian soldiers around them.

They turned to face the javelins of the Macedonians and went on slowly backing away, trumpeting in fear. Alexander surrounded the whole enemy line with his cavalry and the Indian army was slaughtered.

Porus refused to surrender even though he was weak from his wounds and loss of blood. Only when Alexander, who had seen his courage, sent an Indian called Meroes to ask him not to sacrifice his life in vain, did he surrender.

The battle at the Hydaspes was over within a day. As many as 12,000 Indians were killed, 9,000 others and 80 elephants were captured. In contrast, Alexander had lost just 1,000 men.

It was perhaps the most glorious of his victories and certainly, tactically, he had fought a perfect set-piece battle. The way was now open for Alexander to march his army across India. But where was it to lead?

It led to mutiny, to anger and to perhaps the most courageous act of his life.

ABOVE *King Porus of India, a huge man, leads his army into battle against Alexander and his men.*

BUCEPHALUS

After the battle with Porus, Bucephalus died. Most say it was as a result of wounds received in the battle and that he lingered for some time before dying. Others say that he simply died of old age. He would have been about 30 by this time and had marched and fought for almost all of that time.

Alexander went into mourning for he felt he had lost a dear friend. No one else had ever ridden Bucephalus because he would only allow Alexander to mount. Arrian describes him as "strong and beautiful in body and of a generous spirit. He was black with a white mark on his forehead, not unlike those which oxen often bear. Once during the march between Susa and Persepolis, Alexander lost him. Alexander issued a proclamation that unless the people there would restore him, he would put them all to the sword. He was immediately returned. So dear was he to Alexander and so terrible was Alexander to the barbarians."

Upon Bucephalus' death a huge monument was built (which can still be seen today) and the city of Bucephala was founded.

CHAPTER 10

THE FINAL JOURNEY

IT WAS AFTER THE TERRIBLE BATTLE OF HYDASPES, WHEN ALEXANDER'S FORCES HAD BEEN VERY EXTENDED, THAT THE UNEASE AMONGST HIS MEN BECAME MORE SERIOUS - A DISSATISFACTION THAT SIMPLE GESTURES MIGHT NOT STOP.

ALEXANDER WAS TOLD THAT MANY OF HIS MEN HAD
HAD ENOUGH AND THAT THEY NO LONGER WANTED TO FOLLOW HIM
TO THE GANGES OR EVEN ACROSS THE NEXT RIVER. HIS OFFICERS WERE
CONCERNED AND TOLD HIM THAT THEY FELT HE HAD TO LISTEN TO
THE MEN. IT WAS CRATERUS WHO BROUGHT THE SERIOUSNESS OF THE
SITUATION TO ALEXANDER. HE MADE IT CLEAR THAT IT WAS NOT ONLY
THE MEN BUT ALSO SOME OF THE OFFICERS WHO HAD SOME SYMPATHY
FOR THE MEN'S WISH TO GO HOME AND TO STOP THE NEVER-ENDING
MARCHING AND FIGHTING. ALEXANDER WAS FORCED TO LISTEN.

AT FIRST HE WAS VERY ANGRY AND TOLD THEM: "IF YOU WANT TO GO
HOME, GO. I SHALL NOT STOP YOU. AND YOU CAN TELL YOUR WIVES
AND CHILDREN THAT YOU DESERTED YOUR KING WHEN HE WAS
SURROUNDED BY ENEMIES."

HE THEN WENT TO HIS TENT AND LEFT HIS MEN TO CONSIDER WHAT
HE HAD SAID. HE HOPED THEY WOULD STOP LISTENING TO THE VOICES
OF THOSE WHO WERE FOR GOING HOME. HE HOPED THEY HAD JUST
BEEN TEMPORARILY INFLUENCED BY A FEW MALCONTENTS.

Alexander continued to stay in his tent and allowed no one to see him. Surely his men would change their minds ...

Unfortunately, this time they did not. Alexander's men were angry when he lost his temper with them. They were even more angry that he went off to his tent and refused to see any of them. They were now more determined than ever to go home.

While Alexander was hidden from his men he offered a sacrifice in the hope that the omens would be in favour of crossing the river and advancing across India. The omens were not in favour of this decision and so he sent for his companion bodyguard and the senior officers and told them that he had decided that the gods were against going on. He had, therefore, decided to withdraw.

There can be no doubt that the Macedonian soldiers were delighted, and that Alexander had saved face and possible abandonment by claiming that the gods had told him they were not in favour of a further advance.

If the men thought they would just turn in their tracks and go back on the route they had already fought over they were going to be disappointed. Alexander was determined to head down the line of the Indus, which he confused with the possible head waters of the Nile. His sense of enquiry and the desire for knowledge imparted to him by Aristotle when he was a youth, were still strong.

He had a large number of boats and rafts built on which he intended to ferry his army down the Indus to the sea. This was no mean feat since with camp followers and baggage handlers it was an army of around 100,000.

Before they headed south on the river, Alexander ordered vast siege towers to be erected, bridles and bits made for huge horses and weapons made for a race of supermen to be scattered about the countryside. These were to create a sense of fear in anyone who dared to try and come after him. He sacrificed to the gods and selfishly prayed that no one would ever go further than he had.

Alexander ordered Craterus to go to Carmania with part of the army. Craterus marched the men west to the Lake of Seistan, through Arochosia, across the edge of the Lut Desert and south through the mountains to Hormozia at the head of the Persian Gulf. There he would wait to regroup with Alexander who would lead his part of the army in a great sweep down to the Indian Ocean along the Indus and then along the coast to the rendezvous.

If Alexander's men expected the journey to be uneventful they were sadly deluded.

It was on this part of the campaign that Alexander, laying siege to a city on the banks of the Indus, was nearly killed. He had chosen to set an example to his reluctant soldiers and scaled the walls of the city with two companions.

He expected the men to follow after him, but they hung back and Alexander had to choose between being shot by the arrows of the enemy inside the city or jumping to certain death within the walls. He jumped and, landing on his feet, stood with his back to the wall and fought off the attackers. One of them shot him from close range and the arrow went through his breastplate and into his ribs.

Alexander sank to his knees and the attacker rushed up with his scimitar raised. The two companions, Peucestar and Limnaeus, jumped in front of him and Limnaeus was killed. Alexander, still fighting, was clubbed on the neck and sank to his knees again.

At that moment the Macedonians broke through, snatched him up and carried him away. The defenders of the city were slaughtered while Alexander lay in his tent where the arrow shaft was sawn off and then his breastplate removed.

The arrow head was three inches (seven-and-a-half centimetres) long and two-and-a-half inches (six centimetres) wide and was embedded between Alexander's ribs. It was carefully cut out of the king's rib cage and for days he was close to death.

In the days following the scimitar attack when Alexander was battling for his life, he heard a number of his men outside his tent begging to see him. He put on his cloak and went out to them. The anxious and adoring men were delighted when their king walked amongst them.

The army continued down the Indus for seven months until they eventually came to the Indian Ocean. It was July 325BC.

ABOVE *Alexander has an arrow removed from his side by an army surgeon. He lost a great deal of blood.*

THE PHILOSOPHERS

INSET *Alexander met and tested the wisdom of ten Brahmin – Hindu priests.*

Alexander encountered many people on his journey who excited his interest. He was a great soldier, but he still retained the inquisitive nature that Aristotle had encouraged when he taught the young prince.

Plutarch writes of a meeting with ten Brahmin, wise men who were said to have wise and witty answers to any question they were asked. Alexander decided to test them and told them that he would put to death the first man to give a wrong answer and he ordered the eldest to act as judge. The dialogue went like this:

FIRST BRAHMIN

Q: Which are most numerous … the living or the dead?

A: The living, for the dead no longer exist.

SECOND BRAHMIN

Q: Is it the earth or the sea which produces the largest animals?

A: Earth, for the sea is only part of it.

THIRD BRAHMIN

Q: Which is the craftiest of all animals?

A: That which man is not yet acquainted with.

FOURTH BRAHMIN

Q: Why did you urge Sabas, the ruler here, to revolt?

A: I wished him to live with honour or die as a coward deserves.

FIFTH BRAHMIN

Q: Which do you think oldest, the day or the night?

A: Day, by one day.

Alexander was puzzled by the answer.

The Brahmin smiled and said: "Abstruse questions get abstruse answers."

SIXTH BRAHMIN

Q: What is the best way for a man to make himself loved?

A: If possessed of great power do not make yourself feared.

SEVENTH BRAHMIN

Q: How can a man become a god?

A: By doing what is impossible for a man to do.

EIGHTH BRAHMIN

Q: Which is stronger; life or death?

A: Life because it bears so many evils.

NINTH BRAHMIN

Q: How long is it good for a man to live?

A: As long as he does not prefer death to life.

Some say Alexander asked the last Brahmin to judge who had made the most foolish answer and that he then had them put to death. Others claim that he gave them all presents and sent them away without harming them.

At the coast, near the present-day city of Karachi, Alexander ordered a fleet to be built and placed it under the command of Nearchus, a Cretan. The ships would take a great part of the army along the coast while Alexander led the rest on land, in parallel, through Gedrosia to Cophas, then to Carmania where he was planning on meeting with Craterus.

He had planned that the fleet would resupply them and that they would dig water holes at regular intervals along the coast for the men at sea. For the only time in his life he made a fatal tactical error.

In August 325BC, Alexander took his men into the terrible Gedrosian Desert which runs the length of the Indian coastline. The desert was truly awesome yet local people had assured him that he and his men could make the journey. It may be that they had another agenda and saw this march as a way of destroying Alexander's army. Whatever the reason, Alexander lost as many as a quarter of his men in the rock and shale and savage vastness of the Gedrosian Desert.

He and his men marched and struggled on for 60 days and nights. They marched under the burning sun, died from disease, from thirst, from exhaustion and from the hammering heat and starvation. The ships commanded by Nearchus could not make landfall with supplies as they had hoped and the men were driven to kill their mules and horses for food while pretending to the officers that the animals had died of exhaustion. No one would punish the men for the crime – the officers, and even Alexander, turned a blind eye.

The sand close to the shore was too deep for them to wade through and so they had to take a longer route. Gradually they abandoned the carts which carried the sick and the dying. They had to move on as fast as they could to escape the desert.

In some cases flash floods swept sleeping and exhausted men away and drowned them in the desert. The worst suffering was endured by the women and children camp followers. From this march came another version of the legend of the "helmet full of water".

THE HELMET OF WATER

Alexander marched on foot at the head of his men. He was suffering, as they suffered, from thirst and heat exhaustion. He had sent ahead a small party of light infantry to look for water. He wanted to know well before they arrived at any source of water so that he could halt the men a mile or so from the source to prevent them killing themselves by drinking too much.

The light infantry found a miserable trickle of water, scooped up what they could and rode back with it. As they approached Alexander they tipped the precious water into a helmet and gave it to him. Alexander thanked them for their kindness and, in full view of the troops, poured the water into the sand. If any proof was needed of his skill at leading men, this act must provide it.

It was in December 325BC that Alexander and the remnants of his army were reunited with Craterus and the rest of the army in Hormozia after making their way through the treacherous Gedrosian Desert. Craterus was also reunited with Nearchus who had brought the fleet safely to Salmus, Carmania. He then ordered Nearchus to continue with the fleet to the mouth of the Tigris, where Alexander would meet him again the following spring.

Meanwhile Alexander had discovered that many of the men he had placed in positions of power when he first came this way had abused that power. Alexander purged these satraps ruthlessly and replaced them with men he trusted.

When he found that the tomb of Cyrus the Great had been looted, the body desecrated and the treasures that would undoubtedly have been there removed, Alexander was deeply affected and ordered that the tomb be restored. He may well have reflected on the inscription on the tomb which read:

"Oh man, whoever you are, and wherever you come from (for come I know you will) I am Cyrus, who founded the Persian Empire. Envy me not the little earth that covers my body."

Alexander had the man responsible for the desecration of the king's body and tomb put to death.

The army moved on to Susa in Persia, where Alexander married Statira, daughter of Darius, and Hephaestion was married to her sister so that any children would be cousins.

At the same time, Alexander arranged a mass wedding between his Macedonian officers and men and Persian women which he hoped would cement the relationship between the Macedonians and the Persians in the future.

In the spring of 324BC, as he had promised Nearchus, he met the fleet at the mouth of the Tigris where he had another, and the last, city of Alexandria built.

The men were impatient now. The older veterans had been away from wives and children, mother and fathers, their own hearths since crossing the Hellespont in 334BC. It was imperative to get these disaffected men away from the rest of the army. Their unrest might infect the others and Alexander had plans for the others.

Alexander placed the veterans and many of the wounded under the command of Craterus whom he ordered to leave for Macedonia. Alexander was generous in his gifts to these men for they had served him well. He ordered that they were to be honoured in their homes, he gave gold and all their debts were paid off before they left.

At the same time the rest of the troops moved away from Susa and progressed towards Ecbatana in Media. There Alexander had arranged for games and celebrations and for the army to rest before making its next move towards Babylon. Now personal tragedy struck.

Hephaestion, Alexander's dearest friend and lover, caught a fever. He was told by his physician to diet but refused to do as he was told and ate a boiled fowl and drank a huge beaker of cold wine. His fever got worse and he died, just as his physician had warned he would.

Alexander's grief was truly fearsome. As signs of mourning all horses were to be shorn of tails and manes, all the battlements of nearby cities were to be razed to the ground, no music was to

be played and an oracle at the Temple of Ammon commanded that Hephaestion be honoured as a hero and a demi-god.

Alexander took soldiers and defeated a local tribe and massacred all the men from the youngest to the oldest as a sacrifice to Hephaestion. He spent 10,000 talents on Hephaestion's funeral and tomb.

As for the physician whose instructions Hephaestion had ignored, Alexander had him crucified.

As well as reorganizing his army, Alexander kept the fleet on alert and in good shape by organizing games and races for the crews. It was clear that he had plans that did not include an immediate return to either Greece or Macedonia.

Description from the *Iliad*
the Burial of Patroclus, Achilles' Dearest Friend

The sea was still but for a tiny ripple at the edge as it softly rose and fell – breathing. A company of men and mules searched for driftwood and logs. Tall oaks were felled, split and dragged to the shore where Achilles stood.

The corpse was brought in procession, embalmed and sweet smelling, and placed on the pyre. Around it offerings were laid. Two handled jars of honey and oil, four horses, and two of the dead man's dogs were placed beside him. Then Achilles did something terrible. He sent 12 brave Trojan prisoners on the same journey and placed their bodies on the pyre.

The gods sent an eager wind to kindle the fire. The billowing smoke could be seen inside the walls of Troy.

New Persian troops were now enrolled into the older Macedonian units. Each section was to have a Macedonian leader plus three other Macedonians who were paid more than the 12 Persians who had just enrolled.

Suddenly Alexander fell ill. There had been strange portents and stranger happenings. An unknown man was found sitting on Alexander's throne, wrapped in the royal cloak, who claimed not to know what had brought him there – even under torture he could give no explanation.

Alexander became nervous and seemed to be on edge. Despite his illness, he continued to make sacrifice as he had always done and to observe his religious duties which he also encouraged amongst his troops.

He drank late into the night with friends then took a bath, ate a little and slept. He woke with a fever and could not get out of bed. The following day Alexander was carried on a litter to perform his usual libations and sacrifices and then was taken to the men's quarters where he lay until dark.

He gave orders to those who were to begin their march to be ready to move on in three days' time. He would follow by river a day later. He was taken on his litter to a garden and there he bathed and slept.

BELOW *A marble statue of the dying Alexander, from the second-century BC.*

In the morning he chatted a little with his officers in his room and ordered them to report to him the next day. He ate a little, and lay all night in the grip of fever. For nine days he grew weaker, but always prayed and made sacrifice. He saw his officers regularly and continued to give them their orders.

It was now that the fever consumed him. He was now confined to his bedroom. He was growing weaker and asked feebly for his commanders and junior officers to come to him. He did not speak when they filed by his bed, but he lifted his head a little when they quietly greeted him.

Then the men demanded to see him. Some thought he might be dead already, some that he was only sick. There can be no doubt that these men, many of whom had been with him every step of the way, were grief-stricken. The men filed by his bed and from time to time he tried to lift his head in greeting. He knew them all. Two days later he was dead. It was 10 June, 332BC and Alexander was 32 years old.

Their leader was gone and they were left only with a deep sense of helplessness. It was as if the sun had left their sky.

EPILOGUE

Was he a great king?

Was he a great soldier?

Was he a great visionary?

Was he a great man?

As a leader of men Alexander of Macedon was able to take a force of thousands of men on a journey the end of which he had only dreamed of. These tough and experienced soldiers trusted their young king with their lives and their futures and, as far as it was possible, he never betrayed that trust.

Alexander had the skill to know when it was the right time to make himself available to the common soldier. He knew when to go amongst the men after a battle, when to talk to the wounded, when to let them talk and boast of their exploits to him. He knew, by instinct, what they wanted from him. They wanted a man. They wanted a brave man, but they also needed someone who touched them and whom they could touch – someone they could relate to. For when they grew old they could tell their children and their grandchildren … "I once touched the cloak of Alexander the Great" and they knew they would be honoured for it. Alexander knew his men.

He understood that people do not need to be threatened after they had been defeated. It is better to coax defeated people into believing that what the conqueror offers will be better than what went before.

Alexander tried to keep the political systems of the defeated in place and even left in power the politicians who were there before he came. Like his father, he knew how to make his enemies respect him.

Alexander could be totally ruthless. He had no problem with the wholesale killing of some garrisons, the sale of women into slavery, the sacking of some cities from time to time, if it was warranted by the mores of the time. If men betrayed his trust they could expect to die and not to die easily. In this he was a man of his times.

Was he a great general? Alexander was without a doubt helped by the military machine his father had created before his death, but his planning and forethought, his skilful reading of the temper of the enemy and of his own warriors made the decisions he made in the battlefield incomparable. He understood by instinct when to attack and when to feint, where to probe and when to pretend to fall back.

He had honed his army to react in an instant in the confusion and terror of battle and to turn events in a moment.

Was he brave? Alexander was unquestionably brave enough to lead from the front of a battle into the terrible carnage of hand-to-hand fighting. Leaders were expected to expose themselves to the danger that a common soldier might confront but the fact that he was wounded four or five times, at least, attests to the fact that he did not shirk that test.

Did he have a large vision? Absolutely. Alexander hoped that by his conquests he could unite all the people he ruled as one nation. His hope was to break down the perception of the nations and tribes he conquered as separate and to rule them as a unified people without differences of race or state. He wanted them to see themselves as one nation united by a supreme king.

He may never have achieved that vision, but even as he made the journey towards home he was planning his next campaign into Arabia … If he had lived … Who knows how the world might have looked now?

He had a dangerous temper when he had drunk too much. He favoured friends perhaps more than was wise, he was single-minded, not to say arrogant, to the point where, from time to time, he did not consult those around him. He listened to those he trusted but in the end he went his own way. He could be cruel, arrogant and dismissive of women.

Was he great?

He towered over the events of his life and everything and everyone who was part of it … the generals, the kings, the princes, the leaders, the people … were all in his shadow.

BELOW *A carving from the side of Alexander's sarcophagus showing a combat scene between the Macedonians and Persians.*

INDEX

The publishers would like to thank the following sources for their kind permission to reproduce the pictures in this book:

AKG London: 12t, 52, 72, 85; /Cameraphoto: 67, 77; /Peter Connolly: 12t, 115; /John Hios: 32b; /Erich Lessing: 12b, 12r, 12t, 25, 39, 43, 48, 59tr, 59 ml, 61, 124; /Musee du Louvre, Paris: 29

Ancient Art & Architecture Collection: 14bl, 18, 36, 41, 45, 47t, 56t, 70, 90, 91, 96, 96-97, 106b, 123

Bridgeman Art Library: Musee du Petit Palais, France: 14tl

Corbis: 22, 23r; /Paul Almasy: 92; /Archivo Icongrafico, S.A.: 99; /Bettmann: 10t, 15, 16-17, 23ml, 24, 34, 37, 49, 51, 56b, 60 63, 69, 73, 75, 76b, 76t, 79, 81, 82b, 88, 89, 96br, 110, 114, 119, 122bl, 125; /Burnstein Collection: 9, 10t, 14; /Christie's Images: 57; /Hulton-Deutsch Collection: 30, 120; /Mimmo Jodice: 21, 46/David Lees: 33, 95, 101; /Araldo de Luca: 13, 82t; /Gail Mooney: 32t; /National Gallery Collection; By kind permission of the Trustees of the National Gallery: 74; / Chris North; Cordaiy Photo Library Ltd: 83; /Gianni Dagli Orti: 42, 47b, 55, 65, 70-71; /Fulvio Roiter: 10b; /Stephane Ruet: 107; /Kevin Schafer: 11; /Alex Smailes: 86; /Luca I. Tettoni: 109, 112; /Richard Wayman: 102; /Roger Wood: 122mr; /Adam Woolfitt: 117

Mary Evans Picture Library: 26, 86t, 106t

Photos12.com: ARJ: 35, 87; /Albert Arnaud: 64; /Oasis: 58

Every effort has been made to acknowledge correctly and contact the source and/or copyright holder of each picture, and Carlton Books Limited apologises for any unintentional errors, or omissions, which will be corrected in future editions of this book.